✦ *Mitzvah Journal* ✦

פָּרָשַׁת הַשָּׁבוּעַ

Exodus to Deuteronomy

by Roberta Osser Baum

EDITORIAL COMMITTEE

Rabbi Morrison Bial

Rabbi Martin Cohen

Rabbi William Cutter

Rabbi Isaac Jeret

Behrman House

Project Editors: Gila Gevirtz and Sarah Feldman

Book and Cover Design: Dale Moyer

The author and publisher gratefully acknowledge the following sources of photography and art:

Cover: **Creative Image,** foreground; **Richard Lobell,** background

American Red Magen David for Israel, 77; **Bill Aron,** 65; **Creative Image,** 23, 41, 59; **Gila Gevirtz,** 71; **Jewish Theological Seminary, Joseph and Miriam Ratner Center for the Study of Conservative Judaism,** 53; **Richard Lobell/UJA Press Service,** 17

ISBN: 0-87441-681-7

Manufactured in the United States of America

Contents

The Study of Torah

Turn it again and again, for everything is in it; contemplate it, grow gray and old over it, and swerve not from it, for there is no greater good.
—Ben Bag Bag

The object of the whole Torah is that every person should become a Torah.
—Baal Shem Tov

Each Shabbat we take out a Torah scroll—a *sefer Torah*—from the Holy Ark and read a section of it called the Portion of the Week, or *Parashat Hashavua. Parashah* means "portion." Another word for *parashah* is *sidrah.* The first *parashah* of the yearly cycle begins at the start of Genesis, and the last *parashah* is completed at the end of Deuteronomy. Every year we read all the *parashiyot* (plural of *parashah*) in the same sequence. Beginning with the first *parashah,* we continue, week after week, one *parashah* at a time, until we come to the end of the Five Books of Moses.

Our weekly reading of the Torah is divided into 54 *parashiyot.* Because the number of weeks in the Jewish year varies due to leap years, we combine *parashiyot* as needed. We have a standard way of noting the contents of a *parashah* by listing the book, chapter, and verse (sentence). For example, the first *parashah,* called *Bereishit,* includes Genesis 1:1–6:8. This means it is found in the Book of Genesis, chapter 1, verse 1, through Genesis, chapter 6, verse 8.

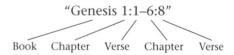

During synagogue services, as the person who reads from the Torah scroll chants the *parashah,* the congregants follow along in a *humash.* A Torah scroll is made of parchment, is all in Hebrew, and has no vowels or punctuation—not even periods! In contrast, a *humash* is a book printed on paper with vowels and punctuation. Additionally, a *humash* has the musical notation, or trope, above and below the words to show how to chant the *parashah,* and it usually has an English translation of the Hebrew text. Most *humashim* (plural of *humash*) not only contain the Five Books of Moses, but also include the selections from the Prophets that we read on Shabbat and holidays. Each of these selections is called a *haftarah.*

By reciting the following blessing each time we begin to study Torah, we are reminded that we are about to perform a holy act, an act that should be done with love, respect, and gratitude.

בָּרוּךְ אַתָּה, יְיָ אֱלֹהֵינוּ, מֶלֶךְ הָעוֹלָם,

אֲשֶׁר קִדְּשָׁנוּ בְּמִצְוֹתָיו וְצִוָּנוּ לַעֲסוֹק בְּדִבְרֵי תוֹרָה.

Praised are You, Adonai our God, Ruler of the universe,
who has made us holy through mitzvot and commands us to engage in the study of Torah.

An Overview of the Five Books of Moses

Genesis בְּרֵאשִׁית

The Book of Genesis begins with the stories of Creation and of Noah and the Flood. It continues with the stories of our patriarchs and matriarchs, Abraham and Sarah—the first Jews—Isaac and Rebecca, and Jacob, Leah, and Rachel. The second half of Genesis is largely devoted to the stories of Jacob and his children. It tells how Jacob was renamed Israel and how his family moved to Egypt, where his son Joseph had become an important official.

Exodus שְׁמוֹת

The Book of Exodus begins with the story of how the children of Israel grew great in numbers in Egypt and were enslaved by the Egyptians. It recounts how Moses became the leader of the Israelites and how, after God sent the ten plagues, Pharaoh let the Israelites go out from Egypt. The physical hardships and spiritual challenges the Israelites encountered when they went out from Egypt and journeyed through the wilderness are described. The Israelites are given the Ten Commandments at Mount Sinai. They are also given instructions on how to build a sanctuary for the tablets of the Ten Commandments, and how to make the seven-branched menorah that would stand in the sanctuary. Exodus also includes many other instructions and laws, such as laws regarding unfair business practices and rules for Shabbat.

Leviticus וַיִּקְרָא

The Book of Leviticus is also known as the Law of the Priests. The priests were a family within the tribe of Levi. They were the religious leaders of the community and conducted all the rituals related to the Temple service. Leviticus describes the duties of the priests as well as those of the Israelites. These duties included participating in the special worship services designated for the annual holidays and observing the holidays according to God's instructions. Leviticus also specifies a legal system to be instituted for promoting social justice.

Numbers בְּמִדְבַּר

The Hebrew name for the Book of Numbers means "In the Wilderness of." The narrative begins about one year after the Exodus from Egypt, after the Ten Commandments were given at Sinai and after many other laws were revealed to Moses in the Tent of Meeting. Numbers includes genealogies of the Israelites and details about the twelve tribes of Israel. It concludes with the arrival of the Israelites at the Jordan River, after forty years of wandering in the wilderness. Across the Jordan lay Canaan, the land God had promised to Abraham, Isaac, and Jacob, which became Israel.

Deuteronomy דְּבָרִים

The Book of Deuteronomy is also known as the Repetition of the Torah. In it, Moses gives his farewell speech to the Israelites before they enter Canaan. He repeats many of the Torah's laws, including the Ten Commandments. He emphasizes that the people would soon enter the Promised Land, should live according to the teachings of Torah, and should pass on its teachings to the future generations. Deuteronomy ends with Moses' blessing for the tribes and with an account of his death on Mount Nebo. Joshua replaces Moses as the new leader of the people.

שְׁמוֹת

Exodus 1:1–6:1

וְאֵלֶּה שְׁמוֹת בְּנֵי יִשְׂרָאֵל הַבָּאִים מִצְרָיְמָה אֵת יַעֲקֹב
אִישׁ וּבֵיתוֹ בָּאוּ...וַיָּמָת יוֹסֵף וְכָל אֶחָיו וְכֹל הַדּוֹר הַהוּא:

These are the names of the children of Israel who came with their households to Egypt
with Jacob...And they died—Joseph, all his brothers, and that entire generation.

(Exodus 1:1, 6)

Highlights from Parashat שְׁמוֹת

Jacob, his sons, and all that generation had died. Their descendants, the Israelites, continued to live in Egypt, and their population grew greatly. Then, a new king (Pharaoh) came to power who did not know about Joseph. Pharaoh told his people that the Israelites might join forces with Egypt's enemies. So he made the Israelites into slaves, forcing them to do hard labor under the supervision of cruel taskmasters.

Pharaoh ordered two Hebrew midwives, named Shifrah and Puah, to kill newborn Israelite boys. The midwives let the boys live. Pharaoh then ordered that all Israelite baby boys should be thrown into the Nile River.

Yocheved,* an Israelite woman, placed her baby boy into a basket and put it in the Nile. His sister, Miriam,* watched as Pharaoh's daughter found the baby. The princess named him Moses and raised him as her son.

When he was an adult, Moses saw an Egyptian beating a Hebrew slave. Moses killed the Egyptian and fled for his life. Moses lived in the land of Midian and married Zipporah, a daughter of Jethro, a Midianite priest. Moses and Zipporah had a son whom they named Gershom.

One day Moses saw a bush on fire that was not being burnt up. God called out to him from the bush and told him: "I will send you to Pharaoh, and you shall free My people, the Israelites, from Egypt." When Moses doubted his ability to do this task, God said there would be signs to persuade Pharaoh to do as Moses asked. Also, Moses' brother, Aaron, would go with him to be his spokesperson, because Moses didn't think he was a good speaker.

Moses returned to Egypt. Moses and Aaron told Pharaoh in the name of God: "Let My people go." But Pharaoh made the Israelites' lives even harder. God reassured Moses that the Israelites would be freed from bondage.

* *Parashat* שְׁמוֹת *does not mention Yocheved and Miriam by name. They are identified later in the Torah—Yocheved in Exodus 6:20 and Miriam in Exodus 15:20.*

Read the Verse

Read aloud the opening verse of *Parashat* שְׁמוֹת and find the Hebrew word for

which the *parashah* is named. Write the name of the *parashah.* _____

Torah Words

הַיְאֹר	בְּנֵי יִשְׂרָאֵל	שְׁמוֹת
Nile, the river	children of Israel	names (of)
הַסְּנֶה	פַּרְעֹה	מֹשֶׁה
the bush	Pharaoh	Moses

In Your Own Words

Read "Highlights from *Parashat* שְׁמוֹת," then retell the story of the *parashah* using the
Torah words above.

Torah Fact

Remember! Each *parashah* is named for the first important word in the *parashah*.
Similarly, each book of the Torah is named for the first important word in the
book. These are the Hebrew names of each book of the Torah:

דְּבָרִים   בְּמִדְבַּר   וַיִּקְרָא   שְׁמוֹת   בְּרֵאשִׁית

Using the above information, name the first *parashah* of each book of the Torah.

_____   _____   _____   _____   _____

Dots and More Dots

Sometimes the dot over the letter שׁ is also the vowel "O" for the preceding letter (מֹשׁ).
Sometimes the letter שׂ has two dots. The dot on the left is the vowel "O" (שֹׂ).
Read each word correctly.

קְדֹשִׁים   גֵּרְשֹׁם   חֹשֶׁךְ   שְׁלֹשִׁם   שֹׁרֶשׁ   מֹשֶׁה

Verses from Parashat שְׁמוֹת

Read these verses from *Parashat* שְׁמוֹת, then answer the questions.

1. וְאַחַר בָּאוּ מֹשֶׁה וְאַהֲרֹן וַיֹּאמְרוּ אֶל פַּרְעֹה כֹּה
אָמַר יְהֹוָה אֱלֹהֵי יִשְׂרָאֵל שַׁלַּח אֶת עַמִּי...

Afterward, Moses and Aaron came to Pharaoh and said to him, "This is what Adonai, the God of Israel, is saying to you: Let My people go..." (Exodus 5:1)

2. וַיֹּאמֶר פַּרְעֹה מִי יְהֹוָה אֲשֶׁר אֶשְׁמַע בְּקֹלוֹ לְשַׁלַּח אֶת יִשְׂרָאֵל
לֹא יָדַעְתִּי אֶת יְהֹוָה...

But Pharaoh said, "Who is Adonai that I should listen to his voice and let Israel go? I don't know Adonai..." (Exodus 5:2)

3. וַיְצַו פַּרְעֹה בַּיּוֹם הַהוּא...לֹא תֹאסִפוּן לָתֵת תֶּבֶן לָעָם לִלְבֹּן
הַלְּבֵנִים כִּתְמוֹל שִׁלְשֹׁם...

That very day Pharaoh commanded..., "Don't give the people any more straw for making bricks as yesterday and the day before..." (Exodus 5:6–7)

You Are There

• You are Moses.

How do you feel demanding that Pharaoh free the Israelites?

_____

How do you feel when Pharaoh increases the workload of the Israelites?

_____

• You are an Israelite.

What do you feel about Moses and Aaron when your work is made harder than before?

_____

A Root: שׁ מ ע

The root שׁ מ ע means "hear" or "listen."

- Write the root. _____ _____ _____   What does it mean? _____ _____

- Read the words built on the root שׁ מ ע.

וַיִּשְׁמַע   שָׁמַעְתִּי   יִשְׁמְעוּ

These words appear in the phrases below from *Parashat* שְׁמוֹת.

- Read each line aloud. Underline the English translation of the word built on the root שׁ מ ע in each line.

1. וַיִּשְׁמַע אֱלֹהִים אֶת נַאֲקָתָם...

And God heard their groaning... (Exodus 2:24)

2. ...רָאֹה רָאִיתִי אֶת עֳנִי עַמִּי אֲשֶׁר בְּמִצְרָיִם וְאֶת צַעֲקָתָם שָׁמַעְתִּי...

...I have truly seen the misery of My people in Egypt and I have heard their cries... (Exodus 3:7)

3. ...וְהֵן לֹא יַאֲמִינוּ לִי וְלֹא יִשְׁמְעוּ בְּקֹלִי...

...but they won't believe me or listen to me... (Exodus 4:1)

Who Was It?

- Who was groaning? _____   • Who heard their outcry? _____

- Who was fearful of being disregarded? _____

Torah Reading

The following verses are taken from Exodus 3. They describe God speaking to Moses from the burning bush.

3 וַיֹּאמֶר מֹשֶׁה אָסֻרָה נָּא וְאֶרְאֶה אֶת הַמַּרְאֶה הַגָּדֹל הַזֶּה מַדּוּעַ
4 לֹא יִבְעַר הַסְּנֶה: וַיַּרְא יְהֹוָה כִּי סָר לִרְאוֹת וַיִּקְרָא אֵלָיו אֱלֹהִים
5 מִתּוֹךְ הַסְּנֶה וַיֹּאמֶר מֹשֶׁה מֹשֶׁה וַיֹּאמֶר הִנֵּנִי: וַיֹּאמֶר אַל תִּקְרַב
הֲלֹם שַׁל נְעָלֶיךָ מֵעַל רַגְלֶיךָ כִּי הַמָּקוֹם אֲשֶׁר אַתָּה עוֹמֵד עָלָיו
אַדְמַת קֹדֶשׁ הוּא:

Become a Torah Reader

This is how Hebrew letters appear in the סֵפֶר תּוֹרָה. There are no vowels in the סֵפֶר תּוֹרָה. Nine of the letters are decorated with crowns drawn as three vertical lines on top of the letter. Look at each letter in turn and say the name of the letter.

א ב ג ד ה ו ז ח ט י כ ך ל מ ם נ ן ס ע פ ף צ ץ ק ר ש ת

Read these words as they appear in the סֵפֶר תּוֹרָה.

...וַיִּקְרָא אֵלָיו אֱלֹהִים מִתּוֹךְ הַסְּנֶה וַיֹּאמֶר
מֹשֶׁה מֹשֶׁה וַיֹּאמֶר הִנֵּנִי

...God called to him from out of the bush saying: "Moses! Moses!" And he said, "Here I am." (Exodus 3:4)

The Mitzvah Connection

All Israel Is Responsible for One Another כָּל יִשְׂרָאֵל עֲרֵבִים זֶה בָּזֶה

During the 1930s and in the early years of World War II, Henrietta Szold, a Jewish American, saved the lives of thousands of Jewish children in Nazi-occupied Europe through her program of Youth Aliyah.

וַיֵּלֶךְ מֹשֶׁה וַיָּשָׁב אֶל יֶתֶר
חֹתְנוֹ וַיֹּאמֶר לוֹ אֵלְכָה נָּא
וְאָשׁוּבָה אֶל אַחַי אֲשֶׁר בְּמִצְרַיִם
וְאֶרְאֶה הַעוֹדָם חַיִּים...

Moses went back to his father-in-law, Jethro, and said to him, "Let me go back to my kinsmen in Egypt and see whether they are still alive..." (Exodus 4:18)

Read aloud the Hebrew verse and its English translation. At first, Moses did not want to return to Egypt to lead the Israelites out of Egypt. But in the end, he accepted the responsibility. Why do you think it is important for Jews to be responsible for one another?

✦ *My Reflections on the Parashah* ✦

וָאֵרָא

Exodus 6:2–9:35

וַיְדַבֵּר אֱלֹהִים אֶל מֹשֶׁה וַיֹּאמֶר אֵלָיו אֲנִי יְהוָה: וָאֵרָא אֶל
אַבְרָהָם אֶל יִצְחָק וְאֶל יַעֲקֹב בְּאֵל שַׁדָּי וּשְׁמִי יְהוָה לֹא נוֹדַעְתִּי
לָהֶם: וְגַם הֲקִמֹתִי אֶת בְּרִיתִי אִתָּם לָתֵת לָהֶם אֶת אֶרֶץ כְּנָעַן...

God spoke to Moses and said to him, "I am Adonai. I appeared to Abraham, Isaac, and
Jacob as El Shaddai, but by My name יְהוָה I was not known to them. I also established
My covenant with them, to give them the land of Canaan..." *(Exodus 6:2–4)*

Highlights from Parashat וָאֵרָא

Moses was reassured that all would go well for the Israelites, and God's most special name was revealed to Moses—יְהוָה. (In prayers, we pronounce this as "Adonai.") God again promised to free the Israelites from slavery and bring them to the Promised Land.

Moses returned to Egypt and told the Israelites what God had said, but they did not listen to him. Moses again begged God to release him from his task of leading the Israelites out of Egypt, but God sent Moses and Aaron back to Pharaoh to tell him to let the Israelites go. God knew that Pharaoh's heart would be hardened against the Israelites. And so, the Bible tells us, God created signs and wonders to convince Pharaoh to change his mind.

The next day the first plague began. The Nile River turned to blood and all the fish died. There was no drinking water, and there was blood throughout Egypt.

Next, the whole country was covered with frogs. Pharaoh said that if God took away the frogs he would let the Israelites go. But when the plague stopped, Pharaoh changed his mind. And so God sent lice to cover both the Egyptians and their livestock. But Pharaoh's heart continued to be hardened.

The fourth plague was insects. Swarms filled the land, except for the region of Goshen where the Israelites lived. Again, Pharaoh would not let the slaves go free. The fifth plague was cattle disease, which killed all the Egyptian cattle but left those belonging to the Israelites untouched. Still Pharaoh would not let the Israelites go free.

Pharaoh remained stubborn even after two more plagues, boils and hail, came down upon his people and his land. And Pharaoh's heart continued to be hardened and he did not let the Israelites go free.

Read the Verse

Read aloud the opening verse of *Parashat* וָאֵרָא and find the Hebrew word for

which the *parashah* is named. Write the name of the *parashah*. _____

Torah Words

מוֹפְתַי	אֹתֹתַי	בְּרִיתִי
My wonders	My signs	My covenant

In Your Own Words

Read "Highlights from *Parashat* וָאֵרָא," then retell the story of the *parashah* using
the Torah words above.

Torah Fact

The Hebrew Bible is made up of three sections: Torah (תּוֹרָה), Prophets (נְבִיאִים),
and Writings (כְּתוּבִים). The first Hebrew letter of each word forms the Hebrew name
of the Bible, תַּנַ"ךְ. On Shabbat morning and holy days we read from the Torah and
from the books of the prophets. The prophets were messengers of God. They brought
hope in times of despair. And, when the people strayed from God's path, the
prophets' words warned them of the consequences of their actions.

A Root: ג א ל

The root ג א ל means "redeem," meaning to liberate.

• Write the root. ___ ___ ___   What does it mean? _____

• Read the words built on the root ג א ל.

גְּאֻלָּה   גּוֹאֲלֵנוּ   גְּאוּלִים   גּוֹאֵל   גָּאַל

• Add the root ג א ל to complete this word from *Parashat* וָאֵרָא.

וְ___ ___ ___ תִּי

God's Promise

- Read the five promises God made to the children of Israel (Exodus 6:6–8), which are listed below.

- Circle the word meaning "and I will redeem."

וְהֵבֵאתִי   וְלָקַחְתִּי   וְגָאַלְתִּי   וְהִצַּלְתִּי   וְהוֹצֵאתִי

- Now read each promise in Hebrew and circle the portion that is the verb.

- Write the word meaning "you" in each promise. _____

1. ...וְהוֹצֵאתִי אֶתְכֶם מִתַּחַת סִבְלֹת מִצְרַיִם...

   ...*And I will bring* you *out* from under the burdens [placed on you by] the Egyptians...

2. ...וְהִצַּלְתִּי אֶתְכֶם מֵעֲבֹדָתָם...

   ...*And I will deliver* you from their bondage...

3. ...וְגָאַלְתִּי אֶתְכֶם בִּזְרוֹעַ נְטוּיָה...

   ...*And I will redeem* you with an outstretched arm...

4. וְלָקַחְתִּי אֶתְכֶם לִי לְעָם וְהָיִיתִי לָכֶם לֵאלֹהִים...

   And I will take you to be My people and I will be your God...

5. וְהֵבֵאתִי אֶתְכֶם אֶל הָאָרֶץ...וְנָתַתִּי אֹתָהּ לָכֶם מוֹרָשָׁה...

   And I will bring you to the Land...and I will give it to you as an inheritance...

The Plagues

In *Parashat* וָאֵרָא we read about the first seven plagues. Read "Highlights from *Parashat* וָאֵרָא" and number the plagues in the correct order.

_____	כִּנִּים	lice	_____	שְׁחִין	boils
_____	בָּרָד	hail	_____	צְפַרְדֵּעַ	frogs
_____	דֶּבֶר	cattle disease	_____	עָרֹב	insects
_____	דָּם	blood			

Verses from Parashat וָאֵרָא

Read these verses from *Parashat* וָאֵרָא. They describe the coming of several of the plagues. Add the correct Hebrew word to complete each verse.

1. ‏...וַיֵּהָפְכוּ כָּל הַמַּיִם אֲשֶׁר בַּיְאֹר לְ_____.

...all the water in the Nile turned to <u>blood</u>.   (Exodus 7:20)

2. ‏...וַתַּעַל הַ _____ וַתְּכַס אֶת אֶרֶץ מִצְרָיִם.

...the <u>frogs</u> came up and covered the land of Egypt.   (Exodus 8:2)

3. ‏...וַיָּבֹא _____ כָּבֵד בֵּיתָה פַּרְעֹה...וּבְכָל אֶרֶץ מִצְרַיִם...

...huge swarms of <u>insects</u> invaded Pharaoh's house...and the entire land of Egypt...
(Exodus 8:20)

4. ‏...וַיְהִי _____ אֲבַעְבֻּעֹת פֹּרֵחַ בָּאָדָם וּבַבְּהֵמָה.

...and there was a terrible skin disease that made human beings and animals break out
in <u>boils</u>.   (Exodus 9:10)

5. ‏...וַיַּמְטֵר יְהֹוָה _____ עַל אֶרֶץ מִצְרָיִם.

...and Adonai made it rain down <u>hail</u> on the land of Egypt.   (Exodus 9:23)

Torah Reading

The following verses are taken from Exodus 7. They describe God's command to Moses to warn Pharaoh that the waters of Egypt would turn to blood because he did not heed God's command: "Let My people go."

16 ‏וְאָמַרְתָּ אֵלָיו יְהֹוָה אֱלֹהֵי הָעִבְרִים שְׁלָחַנִי אֵלֶיךָ לֵאמֹר
שַׁלַּח אֶת עַמִּי וְיַעַבְדֻנִי בַּמִּדְבָּר וְהִנֵּה לֹא שָׁמַעְתָּ עַד כֹּה:
17 ‏כֹּה אָמַר יְהֹוָה בְּזֹאת תֵּדַע כִּי אֲנִי יְהֹוָה הִנֵּה אָנֹכִי מַכֶּה
בַּמַּטֶּה אֲשֶׁר בְּיָדִי עַל הַמַּיִם אֲשֶׁר בַּיְאֹר וְנֶהֶפְכוּ לְדָם:

Become a Torah Reader

Read these words as they appear in the סֵפֶר תּוֹרָה.

...שלח את עמי ויעבדני במדבר...

...Let My people go so that they can serve Me in the desert... (Exodus 7:16)

The Mitzvah Connection

Redeeming Jewish Captives   פִּדְיוֹן שְׁבוּיִים

During the 1980s Jewish communities throughout North America and around the world sponsored Operation Exodus, which brought over a half-million Jews from the former Soviet Union to Israel, where they were able to live and practice their religion in freedom.

עֲבָדִים הָיִינוּ לְפַרְעֹה בְּמִצְרָיִם.
וַיּוֹצִיאֵנוּ יְהֹוָה אֱלֹהֵינוּ מִשָּׁם
בְּיָד חֲזָקָה וּבִזְרוֹעַ נְטוּיָה.

We were once slaves to Pharaoh in Egypt, but Adonai our God took us out from there with a mighty hand and an outstretched arm. (Haggadah)

Read aloud the Hebrew verse and its English translation. Our tradition teaches us not to forget that we were once slaves. As the Torah teaches that God freed us, so, too, must we work to free others—Jews and non-Jews.

פִּדְיוֹן שְׁבוּיִים is the mitzvah of rescuing Jewish captives. One example of this mitzvah is the redeeming of the Jews from the former Soviet Union. For decades, these Jews had suffered from anti-Semitism, poverty, and oppression under the communist governments. With the help of the Jewish communities of Israel and North America, hundreds of thousands of Russian and other Eastern European Jews were able to settle in Israel in the 1980s and 1990s.

How can observing Passover remind you to fulfill the mitzvah of פִּדְיוֹן שְׁבוּיִים?

_____

_____

Think About It!

Do you think that working to build a strong Jewish community is important to being able to fulfill the mitzvah of פִּדְיוֹן שְׁבוּיִים? Why or why not?

✦ *My Reflections on the Parashah* ✦

בֹּא

Exodus 10:1–13:16

וַיֹּאמֶר יְהֹוָה אֶל מֹשֶׁה בֹּא אֶל פַּרְעֹה...וַיָּבֹא מֹשֶׁה
וְאַהֲרֹן אֶל פַּרְעֹה וַיֹּאמְרוּ אֵלָיו...שַׁלַּח עַמִּי וְיַעַבְדֻנִי:

Adonai said to Moses, "Go to Pharaoh..." So Moses and Aaron went to Pharaoh and said to him, "...Let My people go so that they can serve Me." *(Exodus 10:1, 3)*

Highlights from Parashat בֹּא

Moses and Aaron went to Pharaoh once again. They told him that if he did not let the Israelites go, God would bring swarms of locusts that would blanket the land. Pharaoh still would not give in. And so Moses held out his rod over the land as God had directed, and the locusts came.

Pharaoh asked Moses to plead with God to stop the plague. God stopped it but, again, Pharaoh's heart was hardened, and he would not let the Israelites go. God told Moses to lift his arm toward the sky to bring a thick darkness over Egypt. Although the Egyptians could not see anything, the Israelites had light in their homes. Still Pharaoh would not let the Israelites go.

God told Moses there would be one more plague. Moses told Pharaoh that close to midnight the firstborn of every Egyptian would die.

God told Moses and Aaron to tell every Israelite family to slaughter a lamb at twilight on the fourteenth of the month. They were to put some of its blood on the doorposts of their homes, and roast the lamb and eat it with unleavened bread (matzah) and bitter herbs (maror). This was to be a passover offering to God. For on that night, God would strike down every firstborn in Egypt, both human and beast. But God would pass over the houses of the Israelites—the houses that had blood on their doorposts—so that the plague would not strike there. God declared this day a time of remembrance, to be observed for all time.

And so, in the middle of the night, God struck down all the Egyptian first-born. Pharaoh summoned Moses and Aaron and told them to take the Israelites and leave. The Israelites took their dough before it had time to leaven. They wrapped their kneading bowls in their cloaks and carried them on their shoulders. Along the way, they baked flat bread from the unleavened dough.

Thus, with a mighty hand God redeemed us from slavery in Egypt.

Read the Verse

Read aloud the opening verse of *Parashat* בֹּא and find the Hebrew word for

which the *parashah* is named. **Write the name of the *parashah*.** _____

Torah Words

פֶּסַח	חֹשֶׁךְ	אַרְבֶּה
passover offering	darkness	locusts
	בְּיָד חֲזָקָה	מַצּוֹת
	with a mighty hand	unleavened bread

In Your Own Words

Read "Highlights from *Parashat* בֹּא," then retell the story of the *parashah* using the
Torah words above.

Torah Fact

Each Shabbat, after the Torah reading, a selection from a book of the Prophets is
read. The text is called a *haftarah*, הַפְטָרָה. The term *haftarah* means "conclusion."
A different *haftarah* is chanted each week.

A Root: א כ ל

The root א כ ל means "eat."

- Write the root. _____ _____ _____   What does it mean? _____
- Read the words built on the root א כ ל.

וְאָכְלוּ   יֹאכְלֻהוּ   אֹכְלִים   תֹּאכְלוּ

From Parashat בֹּא

Circle each word built on the root א כ ל, then circle its English translation.

וְאָכְלוּ אֶת הַבָּשָׂר בַּלַּיְלָה הַזֶּה צְלִי אֵשׁ וּמַצּוֹת עַל מְרֹרִים יֹאכְלֻהוּ.

On that night, they shall eat the meat [of the Passover sacrifice] roasted in fire
and eat it with matzot and bitter herbs. (Exodus 12:8)

Seder Plate Symbols

Match the Hebrew and English terms for these seder plate items by writing the
appropriate number next to each English term.

___ apples, nuts, and wine mixture	1. זְרוֹעַ
___ roasted egg	2. חֲרוֹסֶת
___ roasted bone	3. כַּרְפַּס
___ bitter herb	4. בֵּיצָה
___ greens	5. מָרוֹר

Match each item on the seder plate with what it symbolizes.

1. apples, nuts, and wine mixture   ___ The bitterness of a slave's life

2. bitter herb   ___ The coming of the spring season

3. roasted bone   ___ The mortar used to make bricks

4. greens   ___ The lamb that was eaten on the first
night of Passover; the Temple sacrifice

5. roasted egg   ___ An additional Temple sacrifice

Verses from Parashat בֹּא

Read the verses from *Parashat* בֹּא, then answer the questions.

1. וּשְׁמַרְתֶּם אֶת הַדָּבָר הַזֶּה לְחָק לְךָ וּלְבָנֶיךָ עַד עוֹלָם.

And you shall observe this [set of Passover rituals] as a binding obligation on you and
your descendants for all time. (Exodus 12:24)

List three Passover traditions that remind us that we were once slaves in Egypt.

_____

_____

2. וַיֹּאמֶר מֹשֶׁה אֶל הָעָם זָכוֹר אֶת הַיּוֹם הַזֶּה אֲשֶׁר יְצָאתֶם מִמִּצְרַיִם מִבֵּית עֲבָדִים...

And Moses said to the people: Remember this day on which you left Egypt,
the house of slavery... (Exodus 13:3)

Of all the Passover traditions, which one best helps you remember the day we left
Egypt? Why?

_____

_____

3. ...בְּחֹזֶק יָד הוֹצִיאָנוּ יְהוָֹה מִמִּצְרַיִם מִבֵּית עֲבָדִים.

...with a mighty hand, Adonai took us out of Egypt, out of the house of slavery. (Exodus 13:14)

Just as Moses worked as a messenger of God by passing on God's Torah to the
Israelites, each of us can work as God's messenger by helping to free those in bondage
to tyranny, hunger, homelessness, and illness. Describe an action you can take as a
messenger of God.

_____

_____

Torah Reading

The following verses are taken from Exodus 12. They describe how Passover
is to be observed.

16 וּבַיּוֹם הָרִאשׁוֹן מִקְרָא קֹדֶשׁ וּבַיּוֹם הַשְּׁבִיעִי מִקְרָא קֹדֶשׁ
יִהְיֶה לָכֶם כָּל מְלָאכָה לֹא יֵעָשֶׂה בָהֶם אַךְ אֲשֶׁר יֵאָכֵל
17 לְכָל נֶפֶשׁ הוּא לְבַדּוֹ יֵעָשֶׂה לָכֶם: וּשְׁמַרְתֶּם אֶת הַמַּצּוֹת
כִּי בְּעֶצֶם הַיּוֹם הַזֶּה הוֹצֵאתִי אֶת צִבְאוֹתֵיכֶם מֵאֶרֶץ
מִצְרָיִם וּשְׁמַרְתֶּם אֶת הַיּוֹם הַזֶּה לְדֹרֹתֵיכֶם חֻקַּת עוֹלָם:
18 בָּרִאשֹׁן בְּאַרְבָּעָה עָשָׂר יוֹם לַחֹדֶשׁ בָּעֶרֶב תֹּאכְלוּ מַצֹּת עַד
יוֹם הָאֶחָד וְעֶשְׂרִים לַחֹדֶשׁ בָּעָרֶב:

Become a Torah Reader

Read these words as they appear in the סֵפֶר תּוֹרָה.

וּבַיּוֹם הָרִאשׁוֹן מִקְרָא קֹדֶשׁ וּבַיּוֹם הַשְּׁבִיעִי מִקְרָא קֹדֶשׁ...

On the first day [observe] a holy gathering and on the seventh day [observe] a holy gathering...
(Exodus 12:16)

The Mitzvah Connection

Money for Wheat מְעוֹת חִטִּים

The Passover Haggadah instructs "all who are hungry—let them come and eat!" It tells us that matzah—the bread of affliction—is a symbol reminding us that our ancestors were slaves in Egypt and that we are to help those who are poor or hungry. Here a student contributes to a High Holiday food drive.

שִׁבְעַת יָמִים תֹּאכַל מַצֹּת...

Eat matzah for seven days... (Exodus 13:6)

Read aloud the Hebrew verse and its English translation. Matzah is made with wheat. A fund known as מְעוֹת חִטִּים —money for wheat—was established by the ancient rabbis to help provide families in need with matzah for the seder.

As an extension of this idea, we collect money to buy Passover foods for the poor. Additionally, many communities sponsor Passover food drives, at which they collect food they then donate to a Jewish agency within the community. The agency distributes the food to those in need.

Describe three actions you could take to support a food drive in your community. For example, how could you encourage others to contribute food? How could you assist in organizing the delivery of food from contributors to those in need of food?

_____

_____

_____

Think About It!

Why do you think our tradition teaches us to help make sure that all Jews can participate in a Passover seder?

23

✦ *My Reflections on the Parashah* ✦

בְּשַׁלַּח

Exodus 13:17–17:16

וַיְהִי בְּשַׁלַּח פַּרְעֹה אֶת הָעָם וְלֹא נָחָם אֱלֹהִים דֶּרֶךְ אֶרֶץ
פְּלִשְׁתִּים...וַיַּסֵּב אֱלֹהִים אֶת הָעָם דֶּרֶךְ הַמִּדְבָּר יַם סוּף...

When Pharaoh let the people go, God did not lead them through the land of the
Philistines...God led them in a roundabout way through the wilderness at the Sea of
Reeds... *(Exodus 13:17–18)*

Highlights from Parashat בְּשַׁלַּח

Pharaoh changed his mind after he let the Israelites go, and he and his officers chased after them in chariots. Frightened, the Israelites turned against Moses, saying it would have been better to live as slaves in Egypt than to die in the wilderness.

God told Moses to lift his rod over the Sea of Reeds. A strong wind parted the sea, and thus the Israelites walked through. The Egyptians pursued them into the sea. God told Moses to hold the rod over the sea again. He did, and the Egyptian army drowned. The Israelites saw God's power, and regained their faith in God. Moses and the Israelites praised God.

The Israelites began the journey to Canaan. They traveled for three days without water until they came to a place called Marah. But the water was bitter. The people complained to Moses. God directed Moses to a piece of wood. Moses threw it into the water, and the water became sweet to drink.

Leaving Marah, they came to Elim and then to the Wilderness of Sin. But there was no food, and the Israelites complained once more. God promised Moses there would be food. That evening quail appeared in the camp, and in the morning there appeared a food called manna. Each morning, the people collected enough manna for that day. On the sixth day of the week, the people collected a double portion so they would not need to collect manna (to work) on Shabbat.

The Israelites continued to Rephidim. Again there was no water. When the Israelites complained to Moses, God told him to take his rod and hit a rock at a place called Horeb, and water would come out of the rock. Moses did so.

As they went on their way, the Israelites were attacked from the rear by the army of Amalek. Moses told Joshua to lead the battle against them while he (Moses) held the rod of God in his hand. When his hands were raised, the Israelites triumphed; when his hands grew tired and came down, Amalek triumphed. So Aaron and Hur supported Moses' hands until Joshua defeated the Amalekites.

Read the Verse

Read aloud the opening verse of *Parashat* בְּשַׁלַּח and find the Hebrew word for

which the *parashah* is named. Write the name of the *parashah*. _____

Torah Words

מָן	מַיִם	יַם סוּף	הַמִּדְבָּר
manna	water	Sea of Reeds	the wilderness

In Your Own Words

Read "Highlights from *Parashat* בְּשַׁלַּח," then retell the story of the *parashah* using
the Torah words above.

Torah Fact

The *maftir* (מַפְטִיר) is the final *aliyah* of the Torah service. The person who chants
the *maftir aliyah* is the one who will chant the *haftarah*.

A Root: א מ נ

The root א מ נ means "faith."

• Write the root. _____ _____ _____   What does it mean? _____

• Read the words built on the root א מ נ.

אָמֵן   מַאֲמִין   אֱמוּנָה

• Read this verse from Parashat בְּשַׁלַּח. Circle the word built on the root א מ נ and
circle its English translation.

וַיַּרְא יִשְׂרָאֵל אֶת הַיָּד הַגְּדֹלָה אֲשֶׁר עָשָׂה יְהוָֹה בְּמִצְרַיִם וַיִּירְאוּ
הָעָם אֶת יְהוָֹה וַיַּאֲמִינוּ בַּיהוָֹה וּבְמשֶׁה עַבְדּוֹ.

The Israelites saw the mighty hand that Adonai brought against the Egyptians and were
afraid of Adonai; they had faith in Adonai and in Moses, the servant of Adonai. (Exodus 14:31)

The Song of the Sea

Moses and the children of Israel sang a song of praise and triumph at the Sea of Reeds. We sing words from the song during services in the synagogue.

מִי כָמֹכָה בָּאֵלִם יְהֹוָה מִי כָּמֹכָה נֶאְדָּר בַּקֹּדֶשׁ נוֹרָא תְהִלֹּת עֹשֵׂה

פֶלֶא....יְהֹוָה יִמְלֹךְ לְעֹלָם וָעֶד.

Who among the gods [in whom the rest of the world believes] is like You, Adonai? Who is like You, glorious in holiness, awesome of praise, Doer of wonders?...Adonai shall reign for all eternity. (Exodus 15:11, 18)

People and Places

Listed below are the names of people who played a role in the Bible's story of how the Israelites crossed the wilderness. Next to each Hebrew name write the number of the matching English name.

1. Moses	חוּר _____
2. Amalek	אַהֲרֹן _____
3. Aaron	מֹשֶׁה _____
4. Joshua	יְהוֹשֻׁעַ _____
5. Ḥur	עֲמָלֵק _____

Listed below are seven places in the wilderness where the Israelites stopped. Next to each English name write the number of the matching Hebrew name.

_____ Sea of Reeds	מִדְבַּר סִין 1.
_____ Wilderness of Shur	אֵילִם 2.
_____ Marah	יַם סוּף 3.
_____ Elim	רְפִידִים 4.
_____ Wilderness of Sin	מָרָה 5.
_____ Rephidim	חֹרֵב 6.
_____ Horeb	מִדְבַּר שׁוּר 7.

Verses from Parashat בְּשַׁלַח

Write the Hebrew names of the missing people and places.

1. וַיַּסַּע _____ אֶת יִשְׂרָאֵל מִ_____...

Moses led the Israelites out from the Sea of Reeds... (Exodus 15:22)

2. ...וְלֹא יָכְלוּ לִשְׁתֹּת מַיִם מִ_____ כִּי מָרִים הֵם...

...but they could not drink the water from Marah because it was bitter... (Exodus 15:23)

3. וַיִּסְעוּ מֵ_____ וַיָּבֹאוּ כָּל עֲדַת בְּנֵי יִשְׂרָאֵל אֶל _____...

They left Elim and the entire community of Israel came to the Wilderness of Sin... (Exodus 16:1)

4. ...וַיַּחֲנוּ בִּ_____ וְאֵין מַיִם...וַיֹּאמֶר יְהוָה אֶל _____...
הִנְנִי עֹמֵד לְפָנֶיךָ שָׁם עַל הַצּוּר בְּ_____...

...They camped in Rephidim, but there was no water there....Then Adonai said to Moses,...
"I will stand before you there on the rock in Ḥoreb..." (Exodus 17:1, 5–6)

Miracles

The four verses above are connected to miracles the Israelites experienced in the
wilderness when they lost faith. Read "Highlights from *Parashat* בְּשַׁלַח." What was
each miracle?

1. _____
2. _____
3. _____
4. _____

Torah Reading

The following verses are taken from Exodus 16. They describe the manna God sent
down to feed the Israelites in the wilderness.

4 וַיֹּאמֶר יְהוָה אֶל מֹשֶׁה הִנְנִי מַמְטִיר לָכֶם לֶחֶם מִן הַשָּׁמַיִם
וְיָצָא הָעָם וְלָקְטוּ דְּבַר יוֹם בְּיוֹמוֹ לְמַעַן אֲנַסֶּנּוּ הֲיֵלֵךְ

5 בְּתוֹרָתִי אִם לֹא: וְהָיָה בַּיּוֹם הַשִּׁשִּׁי וְהֵכִינוּ אֵת אֲשֶׁר
יָבִיאוּ וְהָיָה מִשְׁנֶה עַל אֲשֶׁר יִלְקְטוּ יוֹם יוֹם:

Become a Torah Reader

Read these words as they appear in the סֵפֶר תּוֹרָה.

וַיֹּאמֶר יְהוָה אֶל מֹשֶׁה הִנְנִי מַמְטִיר לָכֶם לֶחֶם מִן הַשָּׁמַיִם...

Then Adonai said to Moses, "I will make bread rain down on you from heaven..." (Exodus 16:4)

The Mitzvah Connection

Memory   זִכָּרוֹן

...זֵכֶר לִיצִיאַת מִצְרָיִם.

...a remembrance of the Exodus from Egypt.

(Kiddush)

During the Passover seder we remember the Exodus from Egypt, when we became a free people. By telling the story every year, we make sure that each generation will remember and rejoice in its own freedom and work for the freedom of those who are still oppressed.

Read aloud the Hebrew verse and the English translation. Each Shabbat, when we recite Kiddush, we are reminded that Shabbat is a remembrance of Creation *and* of our Exodus from Egypt. Only a free people can rest and refresh itself. Only a free people can gather openly and easily to celebrate its connection to God. The Passover Haggadah reminds us that it is our obligation to remember and to tell the story of our slavery and our liberation: "We were once slaves to Pharaoh in Egypt, but Adonai our God took us out from there with a mighty hand and an outstretched arm...In every generation we must regard ourselves as if we personally came forth from Egypt."

Describe two traditions or mitzvot that you can observe on Shabbat because we are a free people.

1._____

2._____

Think About It!

Why do you think our tradition encourages us to keep the story of our enslavement and redemption fresh in our memories?

✦ *My Reflections on the Parashah* ✦

יִתְרוֹ

Exodus 18:1–20:23

וַיִּשְׁמַע יִתְרוֹ כֹהֵן מִדְיָן חֹתֵן מֹשֶׁה אֵת כָּל אֲשֶׁר עָשָׂה אֱלֹהִים
לְמֹשֶׁה וּלְיִשְׂרָאֵל עַמּוֹ כִּי הוֹצִיא יְהֹוָה אֶת יִשְׂרָאֵל מִמִּצְרָיִם:...
וַיָּבֹא יִתְרוֹ חֹתֵן מֹשֶׁה וּבָנָיו וְאִשְׁתּוֹ אֶל מֹשֶׁה אֶל הַמִּדְבָּר...

Jethro, the priest of Midian who was Moses' father-in-law, heard of all that God had done for Moses and for Israel, the people, how Adonai had taken Israel out from Egypt ...And Jethro, Moses' father-in-law, came to Moses in the desert along with Moses' sons and wife... *(Exodus 18:1, 5)*

Highlights from Parashat יִתְרוֹ

Jethro, Moses' father-in-law, heard how God had brought the Israelites out of Egypt. So, he came to Moses' camp with Zipporah, Moses' wife, and their two sons, Gershom and Eliezer. When Moses told Jethro everything that had happened, Jethro realized that Adonai was indeed the one true God.

Jethro saw Moses acting as a judge for the people, settling their disputes. Moses told Jethro that in doing so, he was also teaching the people God's laws. When Jethro saw the long line of people waiting to speak to Moses, he made a suggestion. Moses should share the burden of his position by delegating responsibility to capable, trustworthy people. These people would become judges, make decisions in all minor disputes, and refer major ones to Moses. Moses did what Jethro suggested.

In the third month following the Exodus, the Israelites entered the wilderness of Sinai. They camped before the mountain,* and Moses went up (the mountain) to speak to God. God offered a covenant. If the people would obey God and keep the covenant, they would be God's treasured people; they would be a kingdom of priests** and a holy nation.

Moses summoned the elders of the people and presented God's proposal to them. The people answered in unison: "All that Adonai has spoken we will do!"

God now told Moses to prepare the people to hear God speak. God would appear to them in three days. Moses led the people to the foot of the mountain, which was covered in smoke. The mountain reverberated. Moses was called to the top of the mountain. When he came down, God spoke the Ten Commandments to the people.

*We do not know the actual location of Mount Sinai.
**Israelite priests, or kohanim, were expected to live in a constant state of holiness because it was their responsibility to care for the Holy Sanctuary and to offer sacrifices to God. In this parashah, the Torah teaches us that by keeping the covenant, all the Israelites would be as holy as the priests, the descendants of Aaron.

Read the Verse

Read aloud the opening verse of *Parashat* יִתְרוֹ and find the Hebrew word for

which the *parashah* is named. Write the name of the *parashah.* _____

 Torah Words

הַר סִינַי
Mount Sinai

אַנְשֵׁי אֱמֶת
trustworthy people
(people of truth)

אַנְשֵׁי חַיִל
capable people
(people of valor)

In Your Own Words

Read "Highlights from *Parashat* יִתְרוֹ," then retell the story of the *parashah* using the
Torah words above.

 **Verses from Parashat** יִתְרוֹ

Through Moses, God offered a covenant—בְּרִית—to the House of Jacob,
the children of Israel. Read the verses from the בְּרִית.

1. וְעַתָּה אִם שָׁמוֹעַ תִּשְׁמְעוּ בְּקֹלִי וּשְׁמַרְתֶּם אֶת בְּרִיתִי...

   And now, if you will listen to My voice and keep My covenant... (Exodus 19:5)

2. ...וִהְיִיתֶם לִי סְגֻלָּה מִכָּל הָעַמִּים כִּי לִי כָּל הָאָרֶץ.

   *...then you shall be My treasure[d people] from among all the nations, for all the earth
   is mine.* (Exodus 19:5)

3. וְאַתֶּם תִּהְיוּ לִי מַמְלֶכֶת כֹּהֲנִים וְגוֹי קָדוֹשׁ...

   You shall be to Me a kingdom of priests and a holy people... (Exodus 19:6)

How do you think a holy people should behave? Why?

_____

_____

A Root: ד ב ר

The root ד ב ר means "speak," "thing," and "word."

• Write the root. _____ _____ _____

What does it mean? _____ _____ _____

• Read the words built on the root ד ב ר.

דִּבֶּר   הַדִּבְּרוֹת   דִּבְרֵי   הַדְּבָרִים   וַיְדַבֵּר

• The Hebrew phrase for The Ten Commandments is עֲשֶׂרֶת הַדִּבְּרוֹת, meaning "The Ten Words" or "The Ten Sayings." Our tradition teaches that the entire Torah, including the Ten Commandments, is the "word" of God.

What is the root of the word הַדִּבְּרוֹת? _____ _____ _____

The Ten Commandments: עֲשֶׂרֶת הַדִּבְּרוֹת

Between God and People

The first five commandments reflect the relationship between God and the people of Israel. Read each commandment. (Exodus 20:2–12)

1. _____ אָנֹכִי יְהוָֹה אֱלֹהֶיךָ אֲשֶׁר הוֹצֵאתִיךָ מֵאֶרֶץ מִצְרַיִם מִבֵּית עֲבָדִים.

I am Adonai, your God, who brought you out of the land of Egypt, from the house of slavery.

2. _____ לֹא יִהְיֶה לְךָ אֱלֹהִים אֲחֵרִים עַל פָּנָי.

You shall have no gods other than Me.

3. _____ לֹא תִשָּׂא אֶת שֵׁם יְהוָֹה אֱלֹהֶיךָ לַשָּׁוְא...

Do not use the name of Adonai, your God, in vain...

4. _____ זָכוֹר אֶת יוֹם הַשַּׁבָּת לְקַדְּשׁוֹ.

Remember the Sabbath day to keep it holy.

5. _____ כַּבֵּד אֶת אָבִיךָ וְאֶת אִמֶּךָ...

Honor your father and your mother...

Between People

The last five commandments reflect relationships between people. Read each commandment. (Exodus 20:13–14)

___ 6. ‏...לֹא תִּרְצָח‏

Do not murder...

___ 7. ‏...לֹא תִּנְאָף...‏

...Do not violate the sanctity of marriage...

___ 8. ‏...לֹא תִּגְנֹב...‏

...Do not steal...

___ 9. ‏...לֹא תַעֲנֶה בְרֵעֲךָ עֵד שָׁקֶר.‏

...Do not lie [in court] about your neighbor.

___ 10. ‏לֹא תַחְמֹד בֵּית רֵעֶךָ...‏

Do not covet [long for] your neighbor's house [possessions]...

Although all the Israelites stood together as one people at Mount Sinai, the Ten Commandments were spoken in the singular instead of in the plural. What do you think was the significance of God speaking to each person individually?

_____

_____

_____

Think About It!

Why do you think the fifth commandment is included in the commandments between God and the people?

Torah Fact

The prophets taught the word of God to the people. Although the Torah describes Moses as the greatest of prophets, his story is in Exodus, Leviticus, Numbers, and Deuteronomy, *not* in the books of the prophets—the *Nevi'im* section of the Bible.

Torah Reading

These verses from Exodus 20 describe how we are to remember Shabbat.

8 זָכוֹר אֶת יוֹם הַשַּׁבָּת לְקַדְּשׁוֹ: שֵׁשֶׁת יָמִים תַּעֲבֹד וְעָשִׂיתָ
9
10 כָּל מְלַאכְתֶּךָ: וְיוֹם הַשְּׁבִיעִי שַׁבָּת לַיהוָֹה אֱלֹהֶיךָ לֹא תַעֲשֶׂה
כָל מְלָאכָה אַתָּה וּבִנְךָ וּבִתֶּךָ עַבְדְּךָ וַאֲמָתְךָ וּבְהֶמְתֶּךָ וְגֵרְךָ
אֲשֶׁר בִּשְׁעָרֶיךָ:

Become a Torah Reader

Read these words as they appear in the סֵפֶר תּוֹרָה.

זָכוֹר אֶת יוֹם הַשַּׁבָת לְקַדְשׁוֹ...וְיוֹם הַשְּׁבִיעִי
שַׁבָת לַיהוה אֱלֹהֶיךָ...

Remember the Sabbath day to keep it holy...the seventh day [of the week] is a sabbath
of Adonai, your God. (Exodus 20:8, 10)

The Mitzvah Connection

Leadership הַנְהָגָה

Sometimes the most important and
difficult job for a leader is to show
others how to cooperate in order to
get a job done. For example, when
members of a band don't cooperate,
the result is noise, not music!

...כִּי כָבֵד מִמְּךָ הַדָּבָר
לֹא תוּכַל עֲשׂהוּ לְבַדֶּךָ.

...because the job is much too hard for just you.
You cannot do it all by yourself. (Exodus 18:18)

**Read aloud the Hebrew verse and its
translation.** Jethro taught Moses that a leader
must appoint capable people to help lead.
Think about your school, your synagogue, and
the government. What are the benefits of shared
leadership?

_____

_____

_____

35

✦ *My Reflections on the Parashah* ✦

קְדֹשִׁים

Leviticus 19:1–20:27

וַיְדַבֵּר יְהֹוָה אֶל מֹשֶׁה לֵּאמֹר: דַּבֵּר אֶל כָּל עֲדַת בְּנֵי יִשְׂרָאֵל
וְאָמַרְתָּ אֲלֵהֶם קְדֹשִׁים תִּהְיוּ כִּי קָדוֹשׁ אֲנִי יְהֹוָה אֱלֹהֵיכֶם:

Adonai spoke to Moses, saying: "Speak to the entire Israelite community and say to them, 'You shall be holy for I, Adonai your God, am holy.'" *(Leviticus 19:1–2)*

Highlights from Parashat קְדֹשִׁים

Parashat קְדֹשִׁים is known by biblical scholars as the "Holiness Code." Just as God is holy, we are to lead lives of holiness. Through Moses, God addresses the whole Israelite community, defining an ethical way of life for the Jewish people. Much of the *parashah* tells us how to conduct ourselves in our relationships with others.

The laws in *Parashat* קְדֹשִׁים are varied. We are told to revere our parents and to take care of the stranger because we were once strangers in the land of Egypt. We are to provide food for the needy. When making judgments, we must treat rich and poor alike. We are

not to rob, cheat, seek vengeance, or bear a grudge. We are to love other human beings the way we ourselves would want to be loved and treated. We are not to insult the deaf or place a stumbling block before the blind.

Throughout the *parashah*, God repeatedly says to the people: "I am Adonai, your God." This serves as a constant reminder for the community as to the source of the laws and as a reinforcement of the people's relationship with Adonai. We had accepted Adonai as our God. We had accepted Torah. Now we had to start living by the holy teachings.

Read the Verse

Read aloud the opening verse of *Parashat* קְדֹשִׁים and find the Hebrew word for

which the *parashah* is named. Write the name of the *parashah.* _____

Torah Words

כָּל עֲדַת בְּנֵי יִשְׂרָאֵל	קָדוֹשׁ	יְהוָֹה אֱלֹהֵיכֶם
the entire Israelite community	holy	Adonai, your God

In Your Own Words

Read "Highlights from *Parashat* קְדֹשִׁים." Explain the significance of each Torah word.

A Root: ק ד שׁ

The root ק ד שׁ means "holy."

- Write the root. _____ _____ _____   What does it mean? _____

- Read the words built on the root ק ד שׁ and write the appropriate word next to

  its description.

קַדִּישׁ   קְדוּשָׁה   קָדוֹשׁ

The blessing said on Shabbat and holy days over a cup of wine: _____

The prayer said by mourners or to divide sections of a prayer service: _____

The third blessing of the Amidah: _____

To Be Holy

Add the root ק ד שׁ to complete this verse from *Parashat* קְדֹשִׁים. Fill in the missing
English words.

וִהְיִיתֶם לִי _____ ׁ_ ְ_ ָ_ ־ כִּי _____ו_ ָ_ ְ_ ־ ים כִּי אֲנִי יְהוָֹה וָאַבְדִּל אֶתְכֶם מִן
הָעַמִּים לִהְיוֹת לִי.

You shall be _____ to Me, for I, Adonai, am _____, and I have set you apart from other

peoples to be Mine. (Leviticus 20:26)

38

Verses from Parashat קְדֹשִׁים

The laws of holiness teach us how to conduct our relationships with others. Read each verse. Answer the questions that follow.

1. לֹא תְקַלֵּל חֵרֵשׁ וְלִפְנֵי עִוֵּר לֹא תִתֵּן מִכְשֹׁל...

Do not curse a deaf person or put an obstacle in the path of a blind person... (Leviticus 19:14)

What other ways can someone be at risk of being hurt emotionally or physically? What can we do individually and as a community to reduce such risk?

_____

_____

2. לֹא תִקֹּם וְלֹא תִטֹּר אֶת בְּנֵי עַמֶּךָ...

Do not take revenge or [even] bear a grudge against your own people... (Leviticus 19:18)

How can a person who bears a grudge or takes revenge be hurt?

_____

_____

3. מִפְּנֵי שֵׂיבָה תָּקוּם וְהָדַרְתָּ פְּנֵי זָקֵן...

Stand up in the presence of the elderly and show respect for old people... (Leviticus 19:32)

Why should we show respect for older people? What can we learn from the elderly?

_____

_____

Torah Fact

In the synagogue, when the Torah reading is completed, a member of the congregation or an honored guest lifts the Torah high and turns it around so that the entire congregation can see the words on the scroll. This honor is called הַגְבָּהָה (raising). Holding the Torah scroll upright, the person then sits down as another congregant or guest rolls the scroll and dresses the Torah. This honor is called גְּלִילָה (rolling).

The Ten Commandments

Read each of the Ten Commandments from Exodus 20:2–14.

1. I am Adonai, your God...
2. You shall have no other gods...
3. Do not use the name of Adonai, your God, in vain...
4. Remember the Sabbath...
5. Honor your father and your mother...
6. Do not murder...
7. Do not violate the sanctity of marriage...
8. Do not steal...
9. Do not lie [in court] about your neighbor.
10. Do not covet [long for] your neighbor's house [possessions]...

Read the following selections from Leviticus 19. They reflect the Ten Commandments.

Write the number of each commandment above next to the similar verse from Leviticus 19.

___ ...לֹא תֵלֵךְ רָכִיל בְּעַמֶּיךָ...

Do not go about gossiping with your own people... (19:16)

___ ...אִישׁ אִמּוֹ וְאָבִיו תִּירָאוּ...

One should fear [respect] one's mother and father... (19:3)

___ ...וְאָהַבְתָּ לְרֵעֲךָ כָּמוֹךָ...

...Love your neighbor as yourself... (19:18)

___ ...לֹא תַעֲמֹד עַל דַּם רֵעֶךָ...

...Do not ignore the spilt blood of your neighbor... (19:16)

___ ...וְלֹא תִשָּׁבְעוּ בִשְׁמִי לַשָּׁקֶר...

Do not swear false oaths in My name... (19:12)

___ ...אֲנִי יְהוָה אֱלֹהֵיכֶם.

...I am Adonai, your God (19:4)

___ ...וְאֶת שַׁבְּתֹתַי תִּשְׁמֹרוּ...

...Keep my sabbaths... (19:3)

___ ...לֹא תִּגְנֹבוּ...

Do not steal... (19:11)

___ ...אַל תִּפְנוּ אֶל הָאֱלִילִם...

Do not turn to idols... (19:4)

___ ...אַל תְּחַלֵּל אֶת בִּתְּךָ...

Do not force your daughter to behave in immoral ways... (19:29)

Torah Reading

The following verses are taken from Leviticus 19. They describe ethical business behavior.

35 לֹא תַעֲשׂוּ עָוֶל בַּמִּשְׁפָּט בַּמִּדָּה בַּמִּשְׁקָל וּבַמְּשׂוּרָה:

36 מֹאזְנֵי צֶדֶק אַבְנֵי צֶדֶק אֵיפַת צֶדֶק וְהִין צֶדֶק יִהְיֶה לָכֶם אֲנִי יְהוָה אֱלֹהֵיכֶם אֲשֶׁר הוֹצֵאתִי אֶתְכֶם מֵאֶרֶץ מִצְרָיִם:

37 וּשְׁמַרְתֶּם אֶת כָּל חֻקֹּתַי וְאֶת כָּל מִשְׁפָּטַי וַעֲשִׂיתֶם אֹתָם אֲנִי יְהוָה:

Read these words as they appear in the סֵפֶר תּוֹרָה.

...אֲנִ֣י יהוה אֱלֹהֵיכֶ֔ם אֲשֶׁ֧ר הוֹצֵ֛אתִי אֶתְכֶ֖ם
מֵאֶ֥רֶץ מִצְרָֽיִם

...I am Adonai, your God, who took you out from the land of Egypt. (Leviticus 19:36)

The Mitzvah Connection

Justice, Righteousness צְדָקָה

It is a Jewish custom to donate tzedakah in honor of those we love and respect. This boy and his teammates contributed money to a tzedakah fund in honor of their coach whose support helped them win the league's trophy. Do you think such tzedakah adds justice to the world? Why or why not?

וּבְקֻצְרְכֶם אֶת קְצִיר אַרְצְכֶם
לֹא תְכַלֶּה פְּאַת שָׂדְךָ לִקְצֹר
וְלֶקֶט קְצִירְךָ לֹא תְלַקֵּט:
...לֶעָנִי וְלַגֵּר תַּעֲזֹב אֹתָם...

When you reap the harvest of your land, do not completely [reap] each field all the way to its corners nor pick up what falls when you are harvesting it...leave it for the poor and for strangers... (Leviticus 19:9–10)

Read aloud the Hebrew verses and the English translation. Today most people live far from farms. Therefore, we give צְדָקָה in other ways. For example, we give canned food and money. What can you do to help the poor?

_____

_____

Why do you think our tradition teaches that we add justice to the world when we give צְדָקָה?

_____

_____

Think About It!

How can studying Leviticus 19:9–10 help us live as a holy people?

✦ *My Reflections on the Parashah* ✦

אֱמֹר

Leviticus 21:1–24:23

וַיֹּאמֶר יְהֹוָה אֶל מֹשֶׁה אֱמֹר אֶל הַכֹּהֲנִים בְּנֵי אַהֲרֹן וְאָמַרְתָּ
אֲלֵהֶם...קְדֹשִׁים יִהְיוּ לֵאלֹהֵיהֶם וְלֹא יְחַלְּלוּ שֵׁם אֱלֹהֵיהֶם...

And Adonai said to Moses: "Speak to the priests, the sons of Aaron, and tell them...to be
holy to their God and not to profane the name of their God..." *(Leviticus 21:1, 6)*

Highlights from Parashat אֱמֹר

God told Moses to speak to the priests, Aaron's sons. They were the spiritual leaders. There were special rules that set them apart from the rest of the community. The priests conducted the rituals and presided over the Sanctuary.

God then told Moses to announce the holy days of the calendar. The first holy day that was proclaimed was the seventh day of each week—Shabbat—a sabbath of complete rest. Then, God proclaimed the holy days that were to be celebrated annually.

God proclaimed that the Festival of Unleavened Bread (Passover) is to be celebrated for seven days beginning on the fifteenth day of the first month of the year. The first and seventh days are to be holy assemblies. (In ancient times, holy assemblies were conducted at the Tabernacle, and later on in the Holy Temple. Today we conduct synagogue services.) On the second day, the first sheaf (*omer*) of the harvest was to be brought and waved. The people were to count seven weeks from the day of the sheaf offering. On the fiftieth day (Shavuot), they were to bring an offering of new grain to God.

God then listed the holy assemblies of the seventh month. These were days of rest with offerings to God. On the first day of the month, there was to be a day of complete rest accompanied by loud blasts (of the shofar). The tenth day was to be a sabbath of complete rest, the Day of Atonement.

The fifteenth day of the seventh month was to be the first day of a week-long holiday, the "Festival of Booths." The people were to live in booths (sukkot) as a reminder that they had lived in them when God brought them out of Egypt. The first day was to be a holy assembly. Then, after the weeklong celebration, the eighth day that followed also was to be a holy assembly.

43

Read the Verse

Read aloud the opening verse of *Parashat* אֱמֹר and find the Hebrew word for

which the *parashah* is named. Write the name of the *parashah*. _____

Torah Words

חַג הַמַּצוֹת
Festival of Unleavened Bread

שַׁבַּת שַׁבָּתוֹן
a sabbath of complete rest

חַג הַסֻּכּוֹת
Feast of Booths

יוֹם הַכִּפֻּרִים
Day of Atonement

In Your Own Words

Read "Highlights from *Parashat* אֱמֹר." Describe the holy days to be celebrated.

A Root: שׁ ב ת

The root שׁ ב ת means "rest."

• Write the root. _____ _____ _____   What does it mean? _____

• Read the words built on the root שׁ ב ת.

שַׁבָּתְכֶם   הַשַּׁבָּת   שַׁבָּתוֹת   שַׁבָּתוֹן   שַׁבַּת

• Add the root שׁ ב ת to complete the phrase.

וֹן_ָ_ _ _ַ_
a sabbath of complete rest

Think About It!

What do you think the significance is of a religious law that requires us to rest one day
each week? What do you think is the advantage of having everyone rest on the same day?

Torah Fact

In ancient times, as described in the Torah, the calendar year began in the spring, in
the month in which Passover is celebrated. According to that calendar, what we now
call the High Holy Days took place in the seventh month.

Verses from Parashat אֱמֹר

Read the description of each sacred day.

1. שֵׁשֶׁת יָמִים תֵּעָשֶׂה מְלָאכָה וּבַיּוֹם הַשְּׁבִיעִי שַׁבַּת שַׁבָּתוֹן מִקְרָא קֹדֶשׁ...

Work may be done for six days, but on the seventh day there is to be a sabbath of complete rest [and] a holy assembly... (Leviticus 23:3)

2. בַּחֹדֶשׁ הָרִאשׁוֹן...פֶּסַח לַיהוָה. וּבַחֲמִשָּׁה עָשָׂר יוֹם לַחֹדֶשׁ הַזֶּה חַג הַמַּצּוֹת לַיהוָה שִׁבְעַת יָמִים מַצּוֹת תֹּאכֵלוּ.

In the first month [of the year]...is the passover of Adonai and on the fifteenth day of that [same] month is the Festival of Unleavened Bread of Adonai. For seven days, you shall eat matzah. (Leviticus 23:5–6)

3. ...וַהֲבֵאתֶם אֶת עֹמֶר רֵאשִׁית קְצִירְכֶם אֶל הַכֹּהֵן...עַד מִמָּחֳרַת הַשַּׁבָּת הַשְּׁבִיעִת תִּסְפְּרוּ חֲמִשִּׁים יוֹם...

...and you shall bring the first sheaf of your harvest to the priest...then count fifty days until the day after the seventh Shabbat... (Leviticus 23:10, 16)

4. ...בַּחֹדֶשׁ הַשְּׁבִיעִי בְּאֶחָד לַחֹדֶשׁ יִהְיֶה לָכֶם שַׁבָּתוֹן זִכְרוֹן תְּרוּעָה מִקְרָא קֹדֶשׁ.

...In the seventh month, on the first day, you shall have a day of rest commemorated with a blast [of horns], a holy assembly. (Leviticus 23:24)

5. אַךְ בֶּעָשׂוֹר לַחֹדֶשׁ הַשְּׁבִיעִי הַזֶּה יוֹם הַכִּפֻּרִים...

However, on the tenth day of this seventh month is the Day of Atonement... (Leviticus 23:27)

6. ...בַּחֲמִשָּׁה עָשָׂר יוֹם לַחֹדֶשׁ הַשְּׁבִיעִי הַזֶּה חַג הַסֻּכּוֹת שִׁבְעַת יָמִים לַיהוָה...בַּיּוֹם הַשְּׁמִינִי מִקְרָא קֹדֶשׁ יִהְיֶה לָכֶם... עֲצֶרֶת הִוא...

...On the fifteenth day of this seventh month there shall be [observed] the Festival of Booths to Adonai for seven days...on the eighth day you shall [observe] a sacred assembly...it is the conclusion [of the festival]... (Leviticus 23:34, 36)

What holidays are described in Leviticus 23:24 and 23:27? Describe two traditions we observe on these holy days.

_____

_____

_____

Roots

Write the Hebrew root above the words:
- meaning "rest" in selections 1, 3, and 4.
- meaning "holy" in selections 1, 4, and 6.
- meaning "eat" in selection 2.

Torah Reading

The following verses are taken from Leviticus 23. They describe some of the laws of Sukkot.

40 וּלְקַחְתֶּם לָכֶם בַּיּוֹם הָרִאשׁוֹן פְּרִי עֵץ הָדָר כַּפֹּת תְּמָרִים וַעֲנַף עֵץ עָבֹת וְעַרְבֵי נָחַל וּשְׂמַחְתֶּם לִפְנֵי יְהוָה אֱלֹהֵיכֶם שִׁבְעַת

41 יָמִים: וְחַגֹּתֶם אֹתוֹ חַג לַיהוָה שִׁבְעַת יָמִים בַּשָּׁנָה חֻקַּת עוֹלָם

42 לְדֹרֹתֵיכֶם בַּחֹדֶשׁ הַשְּׁבִיעִי תָּחֹגּוּ אֹתוֹ: בַּסֻּכֹּת תֵּשְׁבוּ שִׁבְעַת יָמִים...

Become a Torah Reader

Read these words as they appear in the סֵפֶר תּוֹרָה.

...פְּרִי עֵץ הָדָר כַּפֹּת תְּמָרִים וַעֲנַף עֵץ עָבֹת וְעַרְבֵי נָחַל וּשְׂמַחְתֶּם לִפְנֵי יהוה אֱלֹהֵיכֶם שִׁבְעַת יָמִים

[On the first day, you shall take] the fruit of the hadar tree [etrog], palm fronds, branches of the avot tree [myrtle] and willow twigs of the brook and you shall rejoice before Adonai, your God, for seven days. (Leviticus 23:40)

The Mitzvah Connection

Observing the Holidays שְׁמִירַת הַחַגִּים

Sometimes the clothes we wear can help make us feel part of a group, as when we wear a sports uniform. A kippah and tallit can be thought of as a Jewish prayer uniform. Do you think that wearing a kippah and/or tallit during Shabbat and holiday services can strengthen a person's ties to our people and traditions? Why or why not?

אֵלֶּה מוֹעֲדֵי יְהֹוָה מִקְרָאֵי קֹדֶשׁ
אֲשֶׁר תִּקְרְאוּ אֹתָם בְּמוֹעֲדָם.

These are the festival times of Adonai, holy assemblies which you are to proclaim, each at its appropriate time. (Leviticus 23:4)

Read aloud the Hebrew verse and its English translation.
Celebrating each holiday helps us identify with our history and our people. It can help strengthen our commitment to our community's values and traditions.

Which national holiday strengthens your identity as a citizen of this country? Why?

_____

_____

_____

Which Jewish holiday strengthens your identity as a Jew? Why?

_____

_____

_____

✦ *My Reflections on the Parashah* ✦

שְׁלַח-לְךָ

Numbers 13:1–15:41

וַיְדַבֵּר יְהוָֹה אֶל מֹשֶׁה לֵּאמֹר: שְׁלַח-לְךָ אֲנָשִׁים וְיָתֻרוּ
אֶת אֶרֶץ כְּנַעַן אֲשֶׁר אֲנִי נֹתֵן לִבְנֵי יִשְׂרָאֵל אִישׁ אֶחָד
אִישׁ אֶחָד לְמַטֵּה אֲבֹתָיו תִּשְׁלָחוּ כֹּל נָשִׂיא בָהֶם:

Adonai spoke to Moses, saying, "Send men to scout out the land of Canaan that I am giving to the children of Israel. Send one man from each ancestral tribe, each one being a prince of his tribe." *(Numbers 13:1–2)*

Highlights from Parashat שְׁלַח-לְךָ

God told Moses to send scouts to Canaan, one leader from each tribe. Moses told the scouts to seek information about Canaan—whether or not the towns were fortified and the inhabitants strong and numerous. They were to bring back fruit of the land. After forty days, the scouts returned with grapes, pomegranates, and figs.

The scouts said the land was good—flowing with milk and honey, as God had said. But, they reported, the inhabitants were fierce, and the cities were fortified. Only one scout, Caleb, was confident the Israelites could conquer them. The others feared that the inhabitants were stronger than the Israelites. So they spread a false report, saying that all the inhabitants they had seen were men of great size; that the scouts looked like grasshoppers in comparison to them.

The people cried and said they wanted to return to Egypt. Caleb and another scout, Joshua (who was Moses' assistant), told the people that God was with them and that they would conquer the land.

God was angered by the Israelites' loss of faith. Moses pleaded with God not to turn against the people. God pardoned them but decreed that the generation that was born in slavery would wander in the wilderness for forty years and die there. Only their children, who were born in freedom, and Caleb and Joshua would enter Canaan.

God directed Moses to tell the people to make fringes—*tzitzit*—on the corners of their garments. The fringes were to remind them to observe God's commandments.

Read the Verse

Read aloud the opening verse of *Parashat* שְׁלַח-לְךָ and find the Hebrew words

for which the *parashah* is named. Write the name of the *parashah.* _____

Torah Words

אַרְבָּעִים יוֹם	לָתוּר אֶת הָאָרֶץ	שְׁלַח-לְךָ אֲנָשִׁים
forty days	to scout (to spy out) the land	send men
צִיצָת	אַרְבָּעִים שָׁנָה	חֲגָבִים
fringes	forty years	grasshoppers

In Your Own Words

Read "Highlights from *Parashat* שְׁלַח-לְךָ". Use the Torah words to retell the story of
the scouts. Who were the scouts? What kind of information were they looking for?
What did they bring back from their assignment? What did they report to the people?

A Root: שׁ ל ח

The root שׁ ל ח means "send."

• Write the root. _____ _____ _____ What does it mean? _____

• Read the words built on the root שׁ ל ח.

שָׁלַח תִּשְׁלָחוּ שָׁלַח וַיִּשְׁלַח

• Read the selections below from *Parashat* שְׁלַח-לְךָ. They each refer to the scouts
Moses sent to Canaan. Circle each word built on the root שׁ ל ח.

• Which selection is from the opening verse of *Parashat* שְׁלַח-לְךָ?

1. אֵלֶּה שְׁמוֹת הָאֲנָשִׁים אֲשֶׁר שָׁלַח מֹשֶׁה לָתוּר אֶת הָאָרֶץ...

2. שְׁלַח-לְךָ אֲנָשִׁים וְיָתֻרוּ אֶת אֶרֶץ כְּנַעַן...

3. וַיִּשְׁלַח אֹתָם מֹשֶׁה לָתוּר אֶת אֶרֶץ כְּנַעַן...

Verses from Parashat שְׁלַח-לְךָ

Read the report from the scouts:

1. ...בָּאנוּ אֶל הָאָרֶץ אֲשֶׁר שְׁלַחְתָּנוּ וְגַם זָבַת חָלָב וּדְבַשׁ הִוא וְזֶה פִּרְיָהּ.

...We came to the land to which you sent us and it is indeed a land flowing with milk and honey, and this is its fruit. (Numbers 13:27)

2. אֶפֶס כִּי עַז הָעָם הַיּשֵׁב בָּאָרֶץ וְהֶעָרִים בְּצֻרוֹת גְּדֹלֹת מְאֹד...

However, the people who live in the land are powerful and the cities are fortified and very large... (Numbers 13:28)

3. ...אֶרֶץ אֹכֶלֶת יוֹשְׁבֶיהָ הִוא...

...it is a land that devours its inhabitants... (Numbers 13:32)

4. ...וְכָל הָעָם אֲשֶׁר רָאִינוּ בְתוֹכָהּ אַנְשֵׁי מִדּוֹת.

...and all the people we saw there were people of great stature. (Numbers 13:32)

5. ...וַנְּהִי בְעֵינֵינוּ כַּחֲגָבִים וְכֵן הָיִינוּ בְּעֵינֵיהֶם.

...and we looked like grasshoppers to ourselves and so we were in their eyes. (Numbers 13:33)

What do you think the Israelites concluded from this report?

_____

_____

Think About It!
In what ways did the ten scouts misuse their position as leaders in the community?

Torah Fact

Pomegranates, רִמּוֹנִים, were brought back from the land of Canaan. This word is used to indicate the two silver adornments placed at the top of the wooden rollers of a *sefer Torah*. These רִמּוֹנִים are designed to remind us of pomegranates; just as a pomegranate is filled with seeds, so is the Torah filled with mitzvot.

51

Fringes—צִיצָת

God directed Moses to instruct the people to make "fringes," צִיצָת, on the corners of their garments. Read this verse and circle the Hebrew word for "fringes" each time it appears.

דַּבֵּר אֶל בְּנֵי יִשְׂרָאֵל וְאָמַרְתָּ אֲלֵהֶם וְעָשׂוּ לָהֶם צִיצָת עַל כַּנְפֵי
בִגְדֵיהֶם לְדֹרֹתָם וְנָתְנוּ עַל צִיצָת הַכָּנָף פְּתִיל תְּכֵלֶת.

Speak to the children of Israel and tell them to make fringes on the corners of their garments throughout the generations. And have them put on the fringes of each corner a thread of sky blue. (Numbers 15:38)

Read this verse from *Parashat* שְׁלַח-לְךָ describing the purpose of צִיצָת.

...וּרְאִיתֶם אֹתוֹ וּזְכַרְתֶּם אֶת כָּל מִצְוֹת יְהוָה וַעֲשִׂיתֶם אֹתָם...

...And [when] you look at it [the fringe], remember all the commandments of Adonai, then do [fulfill] them... (Numbers 15:39)

A Blessing

Practice the blessing recited when putting on a tallit, which has צִיצָת.

בָּרוּךְ אַתָּה יְהוָה אֱלֹהֵינוּ מֶלֶךְ הָעוֹלָם אֲשֶׁר קִדְּשָׁנוּ בְּמִצְוֹתָיו וְצִוָּנוּ
לְהִתְעַטֵּף בַּצִיצָת.

Praised are You, Adonai our God, Ruler of the universe who made us holy with Your commandments and commands us to wrap ourselves in tzitzit.

Torah Reading

The following verses are taken from Numbers 14. They describe how the Israelites lost faith when they heard the scouts' report and turned against Moses and Aaron.

1. וַתִּשָּׂא כָּל הָעֵדָה וַיִּתְּנוּ אֶת קוֹלָם וַיִּבְכּוּ הָעָם בַּלַּיְלָה הַהוּא:
2. וַיִּלֹּנוּ עַל מֹשֶׁה וְעַל אַהֲרֹן כֹּל בְּנֵי יִשְׂרָאֵל וַיֹּאמְרוּ אֲלֵהֶם
   כָּל הָעֵדָה לוּ מַתְנוּ בְּאֶרֶץ מִצְרַיִם אוֹ בַּמִּדְבָּר הַזֶּה לוּ מָתְנוּ:
3. וְלָמָה יְהוָה מֵבִיא אֹתָנוּ אֶל הָאָרֶץ הַזֹּאת לִנְפֹּל בַּחֶרֶב נָשֵׁינוּ
4. וְטַפֵּנוּ יִהְיוּ לָבַז הֲלוֹא טוֹב לָנוּ שׁוּב מִצְרָיְמָה: וַיֹּאמְרוּ אִישׁ
   אֶל אָחִיו נִתְּנָה רֹאשׁ וְנָשׁוּבָה מִצְרָיְמָה:

Become a Torah Reader

Read these words as they appear in the סֵפֶר תּוֹרָה.

וַיֹּאמְרוּ אִישׁ אֶל אָחִיו נִתְּנָה רֹאשׁ וְנָשׁוּבָה
מִצְרָיְמָה

They said, each man to his brother [to one another], "Let us head back to Egypt." (Numbers 14:4)

The Mitzvah Connection

Truth אֱמֶת

...וְדַבְּרוּ אֱמֶת אִישׁ אֶת רֵעֵהוּ...

...Speak truth to each other... (Zechariah 8:16)

The truth is not always popular, and it is not always easy to speak the truth. Here Rabbi Abraham Joshua Heschel, himself a refugee from the Nazis, joins with Martin Luther King, Jr., in a civil rights march in Alabama. Both men were committed to speaking the truth about oppression and injustice.

Read aloud the Hebrew verse and its English translation. The unrest and distrust that resulted from the scouts' false reports led to harsh consequences. The people turned against God. They turned against their leader, Moses, and against Aaron, the High Priest. As a result, the Israelites had to wander in the wilderness for forty years.

What gives you courage to speak the truth even when doing so doesn't feel comfortable?

_____

_____

_____

✦ *My Reflections on the Parashah* ✦

פִּינְחָס

Numbers 25:10–30:1

וַיְדַבֵּר יְהֹוָה אֶל מֹשֶׁה לֵּאמֹר: פִּינְחָס בֶּן אֶלְעָזָר בֶּן אַהֲרֹן הַכֹּהֵן הֵשִׁיב אֶת חֲמָתִי מֵעַל בְּנֵי יִשְׂרָאֵל...לָכֵן אֱמֹר הִנְנִי נֹתֵן לוֹ אֶת בְּרִיתִי שָׁלוֹם:...בְּרִית כְּהֻנַּת עוֹלָם...

Adonai spoke to Moses, saying: "Pinḥas, son of Eleazar, son of Aaron the priest, has turned My wrath away from the children of Israel...Therefore, say that I give him My covenant of peace...a covenant of eternal priesthood." *(Numbers 25:10–13)*

Highlights from Parashat פִּינְחָס

Pinḥas was the son of Eleazar and the grandson of Aaron the High Priest. Pinḥas had defended God's law, and God rewarded him with a special pact: his descendants would be priests forever.

As the Israelites came to the Jordan River, God told Moses and Eleazar to take a census of men twenty years old and more. In this census, there was no one left from the previous census taken by Moses and Aaron, except Joshua and Caleb. This was the generation that God had said would enter Canaan.

God told Moses that the land in Canaan was to be divided among the tribes based on their populations. (Land was owned by men, and only sons could inherit from their parents.) The five daughters of Zelophehad protested. Their father had died without a male heir. They asked that his right to property be transferred to them. The Torah teaches

that Moses spoke with God. God agreed with the women and told Moses that property could be inherited by daughters if a man died without a son.

God told Moses to go up Mount Abarim to view the land God had promised the Israelites. God told him he wouldn't enter the land but would die in the wilderness because he disobeyed God at the waters of Meribat-Kadesh.

Moses asked God to appoint a new leader (to take over when Moses died). God appointed Joshua and told Moses to acknowledge Joshua in front of Eleazar and the whole community. Moses laid his hands upon Joshua and designated him as God decreed.

God instructed Moses regarding the sacrifices that should be brought before God daily and on Shabbat, festivals, and new moons.

Read the Verse

Read aloud the opening verse of *Parashat* פִּינְחָס and find the Hebrew word for

which the *parashah* is named. **Write the name of the *parashah*. _____**

Torah Words

יְהוֹשֻׁעַ	נַחֲלָה	בְּנוֹת צְלָפְחָד	כֹּהֵן
Joshua	inheritance/ property	daughters of Zelophehad	priest

In Your Own Words

Read "Highlights from *Parashat* פִּינְחָס." Use the Torah words to answer the following questions.

1. Why was Pinḥas rewarded and how was Pinḥas rewarded?

2. What caused the daughters of Zelophehad to petition Moses for change?

3. What new law came to pass regarding women's right to an inheritance?

4. How did Moses respond when God told him he would not enter the Promised Land?

5. What was Joshua's role to be following the death of Moses?

Think About It!

Upon hearing that he would not enter the Promised Land, Moses immediately asked that a new leader be appointed. What does this tell us about his character?

Torah Fact

Although the congregation stands when the Torah scroll is removed from and returned to the Ark, in most synagogues, congregants remain seated during the reading of the *parashah*. The reason for remaining seated is that the portion of the service devoted to the Torah reading is considered to be a form of study or instruction, and students generally sit when they study.

A Root: נ ח ל

The root נ ח ל means "inherit" and "possess."

• Write the root. _____ _____ _____

  What does it mean? _____ _____

• Read the words built on the root נ ח ל.

נַחֲלָתוֹ   נַחֲלַת   נַחֲלָה

God's Decision

Read the verses below from *Parashat* פִּינְחָס. Circle the two words built on the root meaning "inherit."

וַיֹּאמֶר יְהֹוָה אֶל מֹשֶׁה לֵאמֹר. כֵּן בְּנוֹת צְלָפְחָד דֹּבְרֹת נָתֹן תִּתֵּן לָהֶם אֲחֻזַּת נַחֲלָה בְּתוֹךְ אֲחֵי אֲבִיהֶם וְהַעֲבַרְתָּ אֶת נַחֲלַת אֲבִיהֶן לָהֶן.

Adonai spoke to Moses, saying: "The daughters of Zelophehad spoke correctly and you surely must give them a portion of the inheritance among their father's kinsmen. Transfer their father's inheritance to them." (Numbers 27:6–7)

Verses from Parashat פִּינְחָס

Read the petition of the daughters of Zelophehad.

1.   אָבִינוּ מֵת בַּמִּדְבָּר...וּבָנִים לֹא הָיוּ לוֹ.

Our father died in the wilderness...and he had no sons. (Numbers 27:3)

2.   לָמָּה יִגָּרַע שֵׁם אָבִינוּ מִתּוֹךְ מִשְׁפַּחְתּוֹ כִּי אֵין לוֹ בֵן...

Why should our father's name disappear from his family because he had no son?...
(Numbers 27:4)

The quiet protest of the daughters of Zelophehad established the law of Torah that women would inherit property when there was no son. The daughters names were:

מַחְלָה   נֹעָה   חָגְלָה   מִלְכָּה   תִּרְצָה

On page 58, write a dialogue that might have taken place among the sisters when they first heard that they would not inherit their father's right to property. Include a discussion of how they could ask for the decree to be changed.

_____

_____

_____

_____

_____

_____

_____

Women of Valor

Write the correct names next to each statement.

Puah   Sarah   Tirtzah   Noa   Rebecca   Milkah   Ḥoglah
Leah   Pharaoh's daughter   Rachel   Shifrah   Maḥlah

1. They were our four matriarchs.   _____

_____

2. They defied Pharaoh's order to kill
   newborn Israelite boys.   _____

3. Their protest led to the establishment
   of a new law of Torah.   _____

_____

4. She found Moses in the Nile and raised
   him as her son.   _____

Torah Reading

These verses are from Numbers 27. They include Moses' request when God told him
he would not enter Canaan and a portion of God's response.

יִפְקֹד יְהֹוָה אֱלֹהֵי הָרוּחֹת לְכָל בָּשָׂר אִישׁ עַל הָעֵדָה: אֲשֶׁר יֵצֵא 16
17
לִפְנֵיהֶם וַאֲשֶׁר יָבֹא לִפְנֵיהֶם וַאֲשֶׁר יוֹצִיאֵם וַאֲשֶׁר יְבִיאֵם וְלֹא

תִהְיֶה עֲדַת יְהֹוָה כַּצֹּאן אֲשֶׁר אֵין לָהֶם רֹעֶה: וַיֹּאמֶר יְהֹוָה אֶל 18

מֹשֶׁה קַח לְךָ אֶת יְהוֹשֻׁעַ בִּן נוּן אִישׁ אֲשֶׁר רוּחַ בּוֹ וְסָמַכְתָּ אֶת

יָדְךָ עָלָיו:

Become a Torah Reader

Read these words as they appear in the סֵפֶר תּוֹרָה. They are the words spoken to Moses by God concerning Moses' successor.

...קַח לְךָ אֶת יְהוֹשֻׁעַ בִּן נוּן אִישׁ אֲשֶׁר רוּחַ
בּוֹ וְסָמַכְתָּ אֶת יָדְךָ עָלָיו

...Take Joshua son of Nun—a man [already] possessed with the [divine] spirit—and lay your hand upon him. (Numbers 27:18)

The Mitzvah Connection

Humility עֲנָוָה

וְהָאִישׁ מֹשֶׁה עָנָו מְאֹד מִכֹּל
הָאָדָם אֲשֶׁר עַל פְּנֵי הָאֲדָמָה.

Moses was a very humble man, [more modest] than any other man [person] on the face of the earth. (Numbers 12:3)

For Jewish values and traditions to thrive, older and younger generations must have the humility to listen to and learn from one another. Here a cantor teaches her student how to blow shofar for the High Holidays. What do you want to learn from your elders? What would you like to teach?

Read aloud the Hebrew verse and its English translation. When God told Moses that he would not enter the Promised Land, Moses proved his humility by showing immediate concern for his people rather than for himself.

Putting the needs of others before your own is a sign of humility and shows concern for the welfare of others. Describe an instance when you placed someone else's needs before your own.

_____

_____

_____

✦ *My Reflections on the Parashah* ✦

וָאֶתְחַנַּן

Deuteronomy 3:23–7:11

וָאֶתְחַנַּן אֶל יְהֹוָה בָּעֵת הַהִוא לֵאמֹר: אֲדֹנָי יֱהֹוִה...אֶעְבְּרָה
נָּא וְאֶרְאֶה אֶת הָאָרֶץ הַטּוֹבָה אֲשֶׁר בְּעֵבֶר הַיַּרְדֵּן הָהָר
הַטּוֹב הַזֶּה וְהַלְּבָנֹן:

At that time, I implored Adonai saying: "Adonai, Adonai...please, let me cross over and see the good land on the other side of the Jordan, that lovely mountain [range] and the Lebanon." (Deuteronomy 3:23–25)

Highlights from Parashat וָאֶתְחַנַּן

The *parashah* opens with a continuation of Moses' speech, which began in the first *parashah* of Deuteronomy. In it Moses told the people that God would not allow him to enter the new land. He would only be permitted to view the land, which was on the other side of the Jordan River.

Moses told the people to keep God's commandments and not to add to them or take anything away from them. He reminded them of the time they stood together at Mount Ḥoreb (Mount Sinai), to hear the words of God. He warned them against practicing idolatry, which they would find among the people of the land.

In the second part of his speech, Moses reminded the Israelites that God had made a covenant with them at Mount Ḥoreb—to observe God's laws. Moses once again set before the people

the Torah, the "Teaching" they were to follow. He began by repeating the Ten Commandments. Again and again, Moses implored the people to observe all God's laws and rules.

And then Moses recited the words we now call the Shema: "Hear, O Israel! Adonai is our God, Adonai is One." He continued: "Love God with all your heart, and with all your soul, and with all your might." The Israelites were told to recite these words of Adonai in the evening and in the morning, to teach them throughout the generations to their children, and to write them on the doorposts of their homes. They were instructed to tell their children that they had been slaves in Egypt and that Adonai had brought them out of Egypt with a mighty hand and with signs and wonders. Their story was to be told and retold throughout the ages.

Read the Verse

Read aloud the opening verse of *Parashat* וָאֶתְחַנַּן and find the Hebrew word for

which the *parashah* is named. Write the name of the *parashah*. _____

Torah Words

שְׁמַע יִשְׂרָאֵל	הַתּוֹרָה	הַמִּשְׁפָּטִים	הַחֻקִּים
Hear, O Israel	the Teaching	the rules	the laws

מִצְוֹת
commandments

In Your Own Words

Read "Highlights from *Parashat* וָאֶתְחַנַּן," then summarize the first and second parts
of Moses' speech using the Torah words above.

From the Torah into the Siddur

To complete this verse, which begins the second part of Moses' speech, fill in the
appropriate words and name.

הַתּוֹרָה   בְּנֵי יִשְׂרָאֵל   מֹשֶׁה

וְזֹאת _____ אֲשֶׁר שָׂם _____ לִפְנֵי _____.

This is the Teaching that Moses placed before the children of Israel. (Deuteronomy 4:44)

From the Siddur

We recite the verse above (Deuteronomy 4:44) during the Torah service in the
synagogue. The phrase below has been added to the verse to create the prayer
Vezot Hatorah. Fill in the missing name in the phrase below.

עַל פִּי יְהוָֹה בְּיַד _____.

...to fulfill the word of God through Moses.

Now read Deuteronomy 4:44 with its concluding phrase. What is the name of
this prayer?

A Ritual

When we recite Vezot Hatorah, we hold the *sefer Torah* up high and turn it so that the
entire congregation can see the words of Torah. This is known as הַגְבָּהָה (lifting).

Roots: ז כ ר and שׁ מ ר

The root ז כ ר means "remember." The root שׁ מ ר means "observe."

- Write the root meaning "remember." ___ ___ ___

  Write the root meaning "observe." ___ ___ ___

- Read the words built on each root.

  Write the meaning of the root below each word.

וּשְׁמַרְתֶּם   זָכוֹר   זִכָּרוֹן   שָׁמוֹר   זֵכֶר

_____   _____   _____   _____   _____

The Fourth Commandment

Read the fourth commandment as it is found first in Exodus and then in Deuteronomy. Fill in the missing root letters to complete each verse.

___וֹ____ ___ אֶת יוֹם הַשַּׁבָּת לְקַדְּשׁוֹ.

Remember the Sabbath day and keep it holy. (Exodus 20:8)

___וֹ____ ___ אֶת יוֹם הַשַּׁבָּת לְקַדְּשׁוֹ...

Observe the Sabbath day and keep it holy... (Deuteronomy 5:12)

Torah Fact

The Shema declares our acceptance that God is One: יְהֹוָה אֶחָד.

שְׁמַע יִשְׂרָאֵל יְהֹוָה אֱלֹהֵינוּ יְהֹוָה אֶחָד.

Hear, O Israel! Adonai is our God, Adonai is One. (Deuteronomy 6:4)

In the _sefer Torah_ the letters ע and ד are written larger than the other letters. We do not know the reason for this, but one tradition suggests that the two letters form the word עֵד, which means "witness." When we recite the Shema we become God's witness, testifying to God's oneness.

Think About It!

The Shema is chanted daily during the morning and evening services. Why do you think the Shema is also chanted when the Torah is removed from the Ark?

Verses from Parashat וָאֶתְחַנַּן

The V'ahavta passage follows immediately after the Shema both in the Torah and in the siddur. Read these selections from the V'ahavta passage (Deuteronomy 6:5–9).

1. וְאָהַבְתָּ אֵת יְהֹוָה אֱלֹהֶיךָ בְּכָל לְבָבְךָ וּבְכָל נַפְשְׁךָ וּבְכָל מְאֹדֶךָ.

Love Adonai, your God, with all your heart, and with all your soul, and with all your might.
(Deuteronomy 6:5)

2. וְשִׁנַּנְתָּם לְבָנֶיךָ וְדִבַּרְתָּ בָּם...וּבְשָׁכְבְּךָ וּבְקוּמֶךָ.

Teach them [the words of Torah] to your children and speak about them...when you lie down [sleep] and when you get up [awaken]. (Deuteronomy 6:7)

3. וּקְשַׁרְתָּם לְאוֹת עַל יָדֶךָ וְהָיוּ לְטֹטָפֹת בֵּין עֵינֶיךָ.

Bind them as a sign upon your arm and let them be a symbol between your eyes.
(Deuteronomy 6:8)

4. וּכְתַבְתָּם עַל מְזֻזוֹת בֵּיתֶךָ וּבִשְׁעָרֶיךָ.

Write them on the doorposts of your home and on your gates. (Deuteronomy 6:9)

List two mitzvot you can observe to show your love of God. Why do you think these mitzvot express love of God?

_____

_____

Torah Reading

The following verses are taken from Deuteronomy 6. Part of the text is included in the Passover Haggadah.

20 כִּי יִשְׁאָלְךָ בִנְךָ מָחָר לֵאמֹר מָה הָעֵדֹת וְהַחֻקִּים וְהַמִּשְׁפָּטִים

21 אֲשֶׁר צִוָּה יְהֹוָה אֱלֹהֵינוּ אֶתְכֶם: וְאָמַרְתָּ לְבִנְךָ עֲבָדִים הָיִינוּ
לְפַרְעֹה בְּמִצְרָיִם וַיּוֹצִיאֵנוּ יְהֹוָה מִמִּצְרַיִם בְּיָד חֲזָקָה:

22 וַיִּתֵּן יְהֹוָה אוֹתֹת וּמֹפְתִים גְּדֹלִים וְרָעִים בְּמִצְרַיִם בְּפַרְעֹה

23 וּבְכָל בֵּיתוֹ לְעֵינֵינוּ: וְאוֹתָנוּ הוֹצִיא מִשָּׁם לְמַעַן הָבִיא
אֹתָנוּ לָתֶת לָנוּ אֶת הָאָרֶץ אֲשֶׁר נִשְׁבַּע לַאֲבֹתֵינוּ:

Become a Torah Reader

Read these words as they appear in the סֵפֶר תּוֹרָה.

עֲבָדִים הָיִינוּ לְפַרְעֹה בְּמִצְרַיִם וַיֹּצִיאֵנוּ...
יהוה מִמִּצְרַיִם בְּיָד חֲזָקָה.

...We were slaves to Pharaoh in Egypt but Adonai took us out from Egypt with a strong hand.
(Deuteronomy 6:21)

The Mitzvah Connection

Affixing the Mezuzah לִקְבּוֹעַ מְזוּזָה

וּכְתַבְתָּם עַל מְזוּזוֹת בֵּיתֶךָ
וּבִשְׁעָרֶיךָ.

Write them on the doorposts of your home and on your gates. (Deuteronomy 6:9)

Many symbols, such as the mezuzah, proclaim our commitment to Jewish values. The Israeli flag is a symbol of *ahavat Tzion*, our identification with Israel and the Jewish people. Here the Jewish community of Los Angeles celebrates Israel Day with a parade and street fair.

Read aloud the Hebrew verse and its English translation. The word מְזוּזוֹת means "doorposts." We attach the words of the Shema and V'ahavta to the doorposts of our homes. The verses were once written directly onto doorposts. Over time, they were written on a parchment made from the skin of a kosher animal and placed in a hollow container for protection from the rain and wind. Today, we call those containers מְזוּזוֹת. On the outside of each container is God's name שַׁדַּי, "Almighty," or the letter שׁ representing the name שַׁדַּי.

What do you think the symbolism is of placing the words of the Shema and V'ahavta on our doorposts?

✦ *My Reflections on the Parashah* ✦

שֹׁפְטִים

Deuteronomy 16:18–21:9

שֹׁפְטִים וְשֹׁטְרִים תִּתֶּן־לְךָ בְּכָל־שְׁעָרֶיךָ אֲשֶׁר יְהוָה אֱלֹהֶיךָ
נֹתֵן לְךָ לִשְׁבָטֶיךָ וְשָׁפְטוּ אֶת־הָעָם מִשְׁפַּט־צֶדֶק:

Appoint judges and officers in all your gates [of the cities] that Adonai, your God, is giv-ing to you, to your tribes, so that they may judge the people with righteous judgment.

(Deuteronomy 16:18)

Highlights from Parashat שֹׁפְטִים

Preservation of justice and preservation of nature are the two themes in *Parashat* שֹׁפְטִים. The theme of justice is the major focus of the *parashah*; governing the Promised Land in a fair and just manner was of great importance.

The *parashah* begins with a descrip-tion of the structure and practices of a court system. This system was to be run by judges and officials appointed from each tribe. These officers were to govern the people fairly; they were not allowed to show favoritism in their judgments or to take bribes. Once a case was presented in court, the people were to accept the decisions made by the magistrates and other judicial officers. The *parashah* also outlines the role of witnesses in trials.

When the people settled the land they would be permitted to have a king rule over them if they wanted one. But God would choose the king. The king would have to be an Israelite. The king could not send people back to Egypt, nor

be excessively rich. The Torah was to be the king's guide in how to live and reign over Israel.

The people were to designate cities of refuge for those who accidentally killed someone. The example given is that if a man is cutting wood with a neighbor and the head of his ax flies off the han-dle and kills the neighbor, the man can take shelter in a city of refuge to protect him from relatives seeking revenge. For this man did not intend to kill the neighbor. If, however, a person inten-tionally kills someone, he cannot take refuge.

Toward the conclusion of the *parashah*, the people were instructed not to destroy the trees of a city they were besieging. They could eat the fruit of these trees, but they were not allowed to cut them down. However, they were allowed to cut down trees that did not bear fruit if they needed the wood to defend themselves in battle.

Read aloud the opening verse of *Parashat* שֹׁפְטִים and find the Hebrew word for

which the *parashah* is named. Write the name of the *parashah*. _____

Torah Words

עֵצָה	מֶלֶךְ	עֵדִים	צֶדֶק	שֹׁפְטִים
its trees	king	witnesses	righteousness, justice	judges

In Your Own Words

Read "Highlights from *Parashat* שֹׁפְטִים." Then use the Torah words above to state the laws designed to govern Israel.

A Root: שׁ פ ט

The root שׁ פ ט means "judge," "judgment," "justice," and "govern."

• Write the root. _____ _____ _____

What does it mean? _____ _____ _____ _____

• Read the words built on the root שׁ פ ט.

הַשֹּׁפֵט   מִשְׁפָּט   שֹׁפְטִים

• Read the selections below from *Parashat* שֹׁפְטִים. Circle the words built on the root שׁ פ ט.

• Do you recognize the opening words of the first verse in *Parashat* שֹׁפְטִים? Write the number of the selection here. _____

1. ...וְשָׁפְטוּ אֶת הָעָם מִשְׁפַּט צֶדֶק.

2. ...וְאֶל הַשֹּׁפֵט אֲשֶׁר יִהְיֶה בַּיָּמִים הָהֵם...

3. שֹׁפְטִים וְשֹׁטְרִים תִּתֶּן לְךָ...

68

Our Sources

The pursuit of justice, righteousness, and fair judgment is found throughout the Bible.

- Read each selection below.

- Circle the words built on the roots צ ד ק (meaning "righteousness" or "justice") and שׁ פ ט (meaning "judge," "judgment," "justice," and "govern").

- Which selection is found in *Parashat* שֹׁפְטִים? _____

1. לִמְדוּ הֵיטֵב דִּרְשׁוּ מִשְׁפָּט...

Learn to do good. Seek justice... (Isaiah 1:17)

2. וְיִגַּל כַּמַּיִם מִשְׁפָּט וּצְדָקָה כְּנַחַל אֵיתָן.

Let justice well up like water, righteousness like a mighty stream. (Amos 5:24)

3. פְּתַח פִּיךָ שְׁפָט צֶדֶק...

[When] you open your mouth [to judge others], judge justly... (Proverbs 31:9)

4. צֶדֶק צֶדֶק תִּרְדֹּף לְמַעַן תִּחְיֶה...

Justice, justice shall you pursue that you may live... (Deuteronomy 16:20)

5. שִׂנְאוּ רָע וְאֶהֱבוּ טוֹב וְהַצִּיגוּ בַשַּׁעַר מִשְׁפָּט...

Hate evil and love good, establish justice in [every] gate [of your city]... (Amos 5:15)

Did You Know?
The Book of Judges tells the story of twelve leaders. Deborah was the only woman, and one of the three most important judges. (The other two were Gideon and Samson.) Deborah sat beneath a palm tree in the mountains of Ephraim. When the people had disagreements, they came to her for a fair judgment.

 Torah Fact

Except on festivals or special Shabbatot (plural of Shabbat), the *haftarah* chanted after a Torah reading is called by the name of that *parashah*. The *haftarah* for *Parashat* שֹׁפְטִים is therefore known as *Haftarat* שֹׁפְטִים.

Verses from Parashat שׁפְטִים

Read these verses regarding the selection of a king.

1. ...מִקֶּרֶב אַחֶיךָ תָּשִׂים עָלֶיךָ מֶלֶךְ...

...Appoint a king from among your brethren... (Deuteronomy 17:15)

What might be the benefit of selecting a king from among one's own people?

_____

2. ...וְכֶסֶף וְזָהָב לֹא יַרְבֶּה לוֹ מְאֹד.

...he [the king] shall not amass too much silver or gold. (Deuteronomy 17:17)

Why might a king's concern with becoming rich be problematic for his people?

_____

3. ...וְכָתַב לוֹ אֶת מִשְׁנֵה הַתּוֹרָה הַזֹּאת עַל סֵפֶר מִלִּפְנֵי הַכֹּהֲנִים הַלְוִיִּם.

....He [the king] shall write a copy of this Teaching [the Torah] on a scroll for himself in the presence of the priests of [the tribe of] Levi. (Deuteronomy 17:18)

Why would it be important for the king of Israel to have a copy of the Torah nearby?

_____

Torah Reading

These verses are from Deuteronomy 16. They describe how to judge people within a court system.

18 שֹׁפְטִים וְשֹׁטְרִים תִּתֶּן לְךָ בְּכָל שְׁעָרֶיךָ אֲשֶׁר יְהֹוָה אֱלֹהֶיךָ

19 נֹתֵן לְךָ לִשְׁבָטֶיךָ וְשָׁפְטוּ אֶת הָעָם מִשְׁפַּט צֶדֶק: לֹא תַטֶּה מִשְׁפָּט לֹא תַכִּיר פָּנִים וְלֹא תִקַּח שֹׁחַד כִּי הַשֹּׁחַד יְעַוֵּר עֵינֵי

20 חֲכָמִים וִיסַלֵּף דִּבְרֵי צַדִּיקִם: צֶדֶק צֶדֶק תִּרְדֹּף לְמַעַן תִּחְיֶה וְיָרַשְׁתָּ אֶת הָאָרֶץ אֲשֶׁר יְהֹוָה אֱלֹהֶיךָ נֹתֵן לָךְ:

Become a Torah Reader

Read these words as they appear in the סֵפֶר תּוֹרָה.

צֶדֶק צֶדֶק תִּרְדֹּף לְמַעַן תִּחְיֶה וְיָרַשְׁתָּ אֶת
הָאָרֶץ אֲשֶׁר יְהוָה אֱלֹהֶיךָ נֹתֵן לָךְ

Justice, justice shall you pursue so that you may live and inherit the land that Adonai, your God, is giving to you. (Deuteronomy 16:20)

The Mitzvah Connection

Do Not Destroy בַּל תַּשְׁחִית

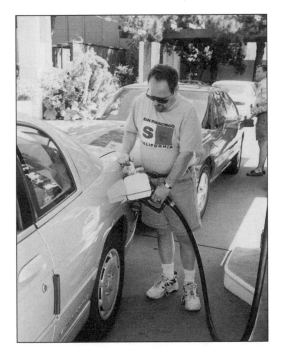

...לֹא תַשְׁחִית אֶת עֵצָהּ...מִמֶּנּוּ
תֹאכֵל וְאֹתוֹ לֹא תִכְרֹת....

...Do not destroy its trees...You may eat of them [their fruit] but you may not cut them down... (Deuteronomy 20:19)

Our tradition recognizes that we need natural resources for almost everything we do: we need wood for houses, water to drink, and gasoline to drive. Our tradition also teaches us to use these resources wisely and sparingly, not wastefully.

Read aloud the Hebrew verse and its English translation. In the Torah, we are instructed not to selfishly destroy what God created. Rather, we are to be the caretakers of Creation. For example, just as people were given the seventh day to rest, we are instructed to permit the earth to rest: "Six years you shall sow your land and gather in its yield, but in the seventh you shall let it rest and lie fallow..." (Exodus 23:10–11).

Describe two ways you can help care for natural resources, such as trees and water.

_____

_____

✦ *My Reflections on the Parashah* ✦

וְזֹאת הַבְּרָכָה

Deuteronomy 33:1–34:12

וְזֹאת הַבְּרָכָה אֲשֶׁר בֵּרַךְ מֹשֶׁה אִישׁ הָאֱלֹהִים אֶת בְּנֵי יִשְׂרָאֵל לִפְנֵי מוֹתוֹ:

And this is the blessing with which Moses, the man of God, blessed the children of Israel before he died. *(Deuteronomy 33:1)*

Highlights from Parashat וְזֹאת הַבְּרָכָה

Before his death, Moses gave a final blessing to the tribes of Israel: he declared, "may [the tribe of] Reuben live and not die..."; he asked God to save Judah from its enemies; and he acknowledged how the tribe of Levi, the priestly tribe, had always placed God first and was responsible for the rituals and teachings of God's law. Moses declared that the tribe of Benjamin, "the beloved of Adonai," would live, protected by God. He blessed the tribe of Joseph by asking that the "precious things of heaven," that is, the rain and the sun, be with them so that whatever they planted would grow and yield produce. Moses compared the tribe of Dan to an agile young lion that leaps across the rocks,

and declared that the tribe of Asher is "blessed above the sons" with good will from the other tribes and with prosperity. Moses concluded by reminding the people that God is the shield and protector of Israel.

Moses climbed Mount Nebo in the land of Moab, and God showed him the land that had been promised to Abraham, Isaac, and Jacob. Then, Moses died; he was 120 years old. The people wept and mourned for Moses for thirty days. Joshua, whom God had designated, became leader of the Israelites.

Never again was there a prophet like Moses among the people of Israel.

73

Read the Verse

Read aloud the opening verse of *Parashat* וְזֹאת הַבְּרָכָה and find the Hebrew

words for which the *parashah* is named.

Write the name of the *parashah.* _____

Torah Words

נָבִיא	וַיָּמָת	הַבְּרָכָה
a prophet	and he [Moses] died	the blessing

In Your Own Words

Read "Highlights from *Parashat* וְזֹאת הַבְּרָכָה," then use the Torah words in your
response to the following:

1. Who received the blessing from Moses?

2. Describe the death of Moses.

Verses from Parashat וְזֹאת הַבְּרָכָה

Read each verse and answer the question that follows it.

1. תּוֹרָה צִוָּה לָנוּ מֹשֶׁה מוֹרָשָׁה קְהִלַּת יַעֲקֹב.

*Moses commanded us with the Torah; it is the inheritance of the
congregation of Jacob.* (Deuteronomy 33:4)

Who makes up the "congregation of Jacob" in each generation? Explain one way the
members of the congregation ensure that their heritage is passed on.

_____

_____

2. ...זֹאת הָאָרֶץ אֲשֶׁר נִשְׁבַּעְתִּי לְאַבְרָהָם לְיִצְחָק וּלְיַעֲקֹב...
וְשָׁמָּה לֹא תַעֲבֹר.

*...This is the land that I swore [to give] to Abraham, to Isaac, and to Jacob...but you shall
not cross over there.* (Deuteronomy 34:4)

Imagine that you are Moses. Describe your feelings on being told that you will not enter the land of Israel.

_____

_____

3. ‏...וַיִּשְׁמְעוּ אֵלָיו בְּנֵי יִשְׂרָאֵל וַיַּעֲשׂוּ כַּאֲשֶׁר צִוָּה יְהֹוָה אֶת מֹשֶׁה.

...and the children of Israel heeded him [Joshua] and did as Adonai had commanded Moses.
(Deuteronomy 34:9)

How would the ready acceptance of Joshua as their new leader help the Israelites?

_____

_____

A Root: מ ו ת

The root מ ו ת means "die."

• Write the root. ____ ____ ____   What does it mean? _____

• Read the word and phrases built on the root מ ו ת.

מֵת   מוֹתוֹ   מֵמִית   וַיָּמָת

• Read the first verse in _Parashat_ וְזֹאת הַבְּרָכָה. Write the word built on the root

meaning "die." _____

• Read the following verse. Write the word built on the root meaning "die." _____

וַיָּמָת שָׁם מֹשֶׁה עֶבֶד יְהֹוָה בְּאֶרֶץ מוֹאָב עַל פִּי יְהֹוָה.

So Moses, the servant of Adonai, died there in the land of Moab, in accordance with the word of Adonai. (Deuteronomy 34:5)

Think About It!
We do not know the exact location of Moses' burial site. Why do you think this was omitted from the Torah's description of his death?

Torah Reading

The following verses are taken from Deuteronomy 34. They describe how the people mourned for Moses and how leadership passed to Joshua.

8 וַיִּבְכּוּ בְנֵי יִשְׂרָאֵל אֶת מֹשֶׁה בְּעַרְבֹת מוֹאָב שְׁלֹשִׁים

9 יוֹם וַיִּתְּמוּ יְמֵי בְכִי אֵבֶל מֹשֶׁה: וִיהוֹשֻׁעַ בִּן נוּן מָלֵא רוּחַ
חָכְמָה כִּי סָמַךְ מֹשֶׁה אֶת יָדָיו עָלָיו וַיִּשְׁמְעוּ אֵלָיו בְּנֵי יִשְׂרָאֵל

10 וַיַּעֲשׂוּ כַּאֲשֶׁר צִוָּה יְהֹוָה אֶת מֹשֶׁה: וְלֹא קָם נָבִיא עוֹד
בְּיִשְׂרָאֵל כְּמֹשֶׁה אֲשֶׁר יְדָעוֹ יְהֹוָה פָּנִים אֶל פָּנִים:

Become a Torah Reader

Read these words as they appear in the סֵפֶר תּוֹרָה.

וִיהוֹשֻׁעַ בֶּן נוּן מָלֵא רוּחַ חָכְמָה כִּי סָמַךְ
מֹשֶׁה אֶת יָדָיו עָלָיו...

And Joshua, the son of Nun, was filled with the spirit of wisdom, for Moses had laid his hands on him... (Deuteronomy 34:9)

Torah Fact

The last letter in the Torah is ל; the first is ב. Together, they spell לֵב, meaning "heart." Torah is the heart of the Jewish people. On the holiday of Simḥat Torah, we read the last verse of Deuteronomy and the first verse of Genesis, symbolizing that the study of Torah is a never-ending cycle.

Deuteronomy 34:12

וּלְכֹל הַיָּד הַחֲזָקָה וּלְכֹל הַמּוֹרָא הַגָּדוֹל
אֲשֶׁר עָשָׂה מֹשֶׁה לְעֵינֵי כָּל יִשְׂרָאֵל.

After completing Deuteronomy and before reading Genesis 1:1, we say in Hebrew, "Be strong, be strong, and let us strengthen one another."

חֲזַק חֲזַק וְנִתְחַזֵּק.

Genesis 1:1

בְּרֵאשִׁית בָּרָא אֱלֹהִים אֵת הַשָּׁמַיִם וְאֵת הָאָרֶץ.

The Mitzvah Connection

Honoring the Dead חֶסֶד שֶׁל אֱמֶת

Our tradition ensures that the memories of our loved ones live on after they have died. For example, we recite the Kaddish prayer for relatives who have died and we contribute tzedakah in memory of their kind deeds. The Israeli ambulance shown here was donated by American Jews in memory of a beloved friend.

וַיִּקְרְבוּ יְמֵי יִשְׂרָאֵל לָמוּת
וַיִּקְרָא לִבְנוֹ לְיוֹסֵף וַיֹּאמֶר לוֹ...
וְעָשִׂיתָ עִמָּדִי חֶסֶד וֶאֱמֶת...

And when the time drew near for Israel [Jacob] to die, he called his son Joseph and said to him... "Deal with me kindly and truly [after I die]"... (Genesis 47:29)

Read aloud the Hebrew verse and its English translation. Jacob's request of his son to deal "kindly" (חֶסֶד) "and truly" (וֶאֱמֶת) with him is reflected in the Hebrew term we use when speaking of the mitzvah חֶסֶד שֶׁל אֱמֶת, "honoring the dead." It is our obligation to deal "kindly and truly" with our loved ones when they die and to bring honor to their memories. For example, on the *yahrtzeit*—the yearly anniversary of a death—a candle is lit that burns for twenty-four hours and Kaddish is recited.

Describe another way we can honor the memory of a loved one who has died.

_____

_____

✦ *My Reflections on the Parashah* ✦